# LOW RATES
# HIGH RETURNS

*'A great and proven way to diversify
into other asset classes.'*

*'The ideas contained in this book are a revelation.
A sensible, low-risk strategy for generating
passive income in the markets, written by two
of the smartest guys I know…who importantly
"walk their talk".'*

# LOW RATES

# HIGH RETURNS

TIMELESS INVESTMENT PRINCIPLES
THE LOW RISK WAY

## PETE WARGENT &
## STEPHEN MORIARTY

Published by:
Wilkinson Publishing Pty Ltd
ACN 006 042 173
Level 4, 2 Collins Street
Melbourne, Vic 3000
Ph: 03 9654 5446
www.wilkinsonpublishing.com.au

A catalogue record for this book is available from the National Library of Australia

Planned date of publication: 06-2020
Title: Low Rates High Returns
ISBN(s): 9781925927269: Printed — Paperback

Cover design by Tango Media based on a concept by Jess Lomas.
Internal design and layout by Tango Media.

**Disclaimer**
This book is written to provide competent and reliable information on the subject matter covered. However, the authors do not operate as licensed financial advisors. This book is written on the understanding that the authors disclaim any liability from the use or application of the contents of this book. The reader should always consult a financial advisor before making any investment decisions.

# CONTENTS

# CHAPTER 1

# THE PROBLEM: RETURN-FREE RISK

## Uncharted territory

We're living through some extraordinary times. For those of us old enough to remember interest rates above 15% and runaway inflation, an era of interest rates at close to *zero* once seemed impossible.

And yet, here we are!

And if financial markets are anywhere near correct, the low interest rate era may be with us for quite some time to come…perhaps even a very long time.

Much has changed in recent decades; whereas once we were expected to retire and live for only a short time in retirement, today it's entirely possible that you might live in retirement for many years, or even decades.

With interest rates globally often stuck at close to zero, many retirees have been forced to eat into their capital.

We used to think of fixed interest investments such as cash and term deposits as delivering *risk-free* returns. But in this respect the world been turned on its head over the past decade or so.

These days, we get the risk of inflation eating away the value of our capital without the worthwhile returns!

Fortunately, there is a better way, and that's what this book is here to help you with.

*In this book, we present a timeless strategy for managing your own money in all markets.*

We believe that your goal should be to continue growing your wealth throughout your entire lifetime — into retirement and beyond. We believe the goal should be to be much wealthier when you pass away than when you retire, so that you can leave a legacy.

Compound growth is known to be the most powerful force in the financial universe, so it makes sense to continue using it to your own benefit for as long as possible. The asset class that has the proven track record for delivering both income and growth is equities. Which is to say, the stock market.

Traditionally, older investors have shied away from the volatility of the stock market in favour of the predictable safety of cash, fixed interest investments, or annuities. But the low interest rate era has forced many to have a rethink. Is it possible to consistently generate acceptable returns from stock markets without the risk? It is, but it may require thinking a little differently from what the finance industry typically recommends that you do.

Fortunately, this short but powerful book is here to show you exactly how to do that.

There's no fluff here: it's a short, sharp book that gets straight to the key points.

## Why we wrote this book

We wrote this book to explode some of the myths about investing, many of which are espoused by members of the financial services industry itself, to benefit themselves rather than you.

This is also a book about *you*.

And why you can manage your own money. As we often say:

*'It's not that hard, honestly!'*

We've found through our personality assessments that there are a few reasons why people seek financial independence. For high achievers, financial success is usually about achieving significance. For more analytical types, learning how to invest tends to be about security.

And for others with a freedom of spirit or a more adventurous bent, becoming a successful investor is more about the freedom to do their own thing. It's a challenge to write a book with the aim of helping different people who have individual personalities, but with some careful thought, we've managed to do it.

Our goal is to help you understand markets sufficiently to implement our systematic approach and manage your own finances, or at least to seek further information so that you can. Understanding your personality traits and motivations is still important because it helps you to recognise your behavioural traits and their potential flaws (we all have them) and the related risks.

Few books account for these differences. The good news is that it takes all sorts.

*The strategies we present in this book are timeless and can be used by anyone.*

We have included a questionnaire to determine what sort of personality you have, and how that influences that way you invest. We have also endeavoured to keep the strategy simple.

As Einstein once said: '*Make it simple, but no simpler*'. We have made additional suggestions for experienced investors to aid in understanding the emotions attached to investing.

Ed Thorp said that he only invested once he became emotionally comfortable with his current position.

*We want to show you how to do the same, and to generate stronger than average returns on your capital, with lower than average risk.*

## A bit about Stephen

I've been an investor for 20 years, and a committed full-time investor for approximately a dozen of those years. I bought my first stock around 1980 — a small company called Pivot Group, which, if I remember correctly, was on the Sydney Seconds Board, before the ASX was born. Needless to say, it was a tip from a work colleague, and as it turned out, not a very good one.

Back then I thought buying stock tips was a thrilling way to make money. It was like going to the races — gossip, speculation, excitement — all combined in one place. After that resounding failure, I did what most do and worked for a living.

I worked in the private sector, and later I started my own company.

Later again I went to university, worked in the public sector as a political advisor, and in 2005, accompanied my then-wife to Japan as she pursued her career.

While I'd always been an investor, in early 2006, I rekindled my interest in stock markets and economics in earnest.

And with plenty of time to devote to watching and studying stock markets, I read all manner of books, articles and academic papers on the various attributes of stock markets, human behaviour, and natural and social sciences. And I also gained a Masters of Applied Finance along the way.

Like many people, I'd had managed funds where you use a regular payment schedule, sometimes known as dollar-cost averaging, to invest in the stock market. The real action came in 2007 and 2008, when the global financial crisis hit and crashed markets around the world.

It was at this time that I understood the true power of one or two of the most important principles of making successful investments.

*I've made most of my successful investments when markets have crashed or are generally shunned. This includes the global financial crisis and the 2009 recovery, late 2011 with the US banking system, and more recently in 2016 with Brexit.*

These were: *mean reversion* and *buy low, sell high*. I understood that when it comes to stock markets, history does repeat. Like many things in life, stock markets have cycles: short ones, long ones where they go up, then down, then up again…like a tide that comes in and goes out on a longer timescale.

These cycles appear in all stock markets around the world, whether they are in developed countries like Australia, or emerging markets such as Turkey. After seeing these patterns and reading a vast amount of literature on the topic, I understood that you could use these patterns and cycles to make money in the stock market.

It isn't rocket science. It just requires the bringing together of a few timeless principles, and these are discussed in this book. However, I also noticed that the patterns also led to emotional patterns, and these emotions can send you on a rollercoaster resulting in moments of pain mixed with moments of joy.

Emotions tend to be especially strong when markets are in turmoil, so it requires that you can coolly, and in a measured fashion, understand where the stock market cycle is at any given point in time. I also discovered that there is a large body of myths about investing that are just plain wrong.

Like many myths, they *feel* and sound right.

They are mentioned often by mainstream finance commentators and are blindly accepted without much scrutiny. However, if you can think for yourself with an open mind, you soon discover that these myths mislead investors and result in investors making wrong decisions (often at precisely the time they should be doing the opposite).

Over time, I developed the strategy contained in this book, which has delivered above-average returns in many stock markets around the world.

It's not a complex strategy. It's simple and can be implemented by anyone.

As Peter Lynch, a famous investor, said:

*'Everyone has the brain power to make money in stocks. Not everyone has the stomach.'*

By 'stomach', Lynch means emotions. Allowing your emotions to dictate your investment decisions will send you broke in a short space of time…or at least will lose you money.

We'll show you how to understand what type of investor you are — the first rule of life espoused by many sages is 'know thyself' — and avoid succumbing to emotionally-based decision-making when it comes to your investments.

The Japanese have a saying: *Karada ga Oboeteru* — the body remembers. This simply means that after repeated episodes of learning, whether it be karate, tennis or playing a musical instrument, you can see and respond automatically to the events that surround you.

In Western culture, it's sometimes known as 'muscle memory'. Over time, you can gain enough insight and wisdom to be able to respond calmly to the situations that arise in your daily life. It's our hope that if we successfully explain the following principles and strategy, you can gain insight and wisdom for approaching the stock market, and you will see the benefits of managing your own money and becoming a successful investor.

## The aim of this book

This book grew out of the idea that investing is simple, but not easy.

The simple part, unfortunately, comes after the difficult part.

And the aim of the book is to make the difficult part as easy as possible!

*When beginning to take an interest in investing, it's difficult to know where best to start.*

You read a few articles and books, and you think you are getting a handle on it all, but the reality is the more you search for knowledge, the more questions arise. It's an endless loop that can be exciting as you gain more of an understanding but also frustrating as you realise that the loop is indeed endless.

Some questions you might start out with could include the following:

*Am I a long-term investor?*

Most of the finance industry recommend taking a long-term view.

Warren Buffett, the doyen of value investing and one of the world's richest people, always goes on about taking a long-term perspective:

*'My favourite holding period is forever.'*

*Am I a trader?*

Famous traders recommend their own strategies: 'The trend is your friend,' they say.

*Am I a fundamentals guy or a technical guy?*
*Am I a value investor or a growth investor?*
*Should I pick individual stocks?*
*Should I use fund managers or do it all myself?*
*Should I use ETFs or managed funds?*

Here's Steve:

*When I studied for my Masters, the dominant theory was the Efficient Market Hypothesis (EMH). EMH holds that markets are always rational and efficient. But then Warren Buffett retorted that the EMH does not hold true.*

*One thing I did notice is that, like most things in life, everyone talks their book.*

*Most financial industry folks tell you to start early.*

*Like now!*

*"It's time in the market, not timing the market," they say. They say you should ignore the stock market declines because you can't predict them, and so you should just keep putting all your hard-earned cash into the market and sit back and watch it grow.*

*Of course, they seldom declare that "time in the market" is better for them but not necessarily for you. The reason why is because they generate fees, and the less you have invested in the market, the lower their fees are.*

In this book, we will give you plenty of reasons why you should manage your own money. We'll also show you that it's not that hard to identify when markets are cheap or expensive, which can significantly improve your returns. The finance and fund management industry takes a somewhat cookie-cutter approach, nibbling away at balances with their fee structures.

As with many industries, there are rules and regulations, and a good deal of institutional investing is formulaic in the sense that there's little scope for originality.

## Personality matters

A fundamental flaw of the finance industry is the belief that all of us are sensible rational types when it comes to money. And this rationality supposedly extends to each of us when we decide to invest our money.

In our experience, this is far from the case.

> When it comes to money, each of us holds
> different beliefs and knowledge.

Generally, money is a serious business, and no one we know of takes money with a grain of salt, so to speak. However, where we do vary is what we believe about money, particularly what it is for. Some of us think it's for saving as much as possible to provide some sort of security; others have little interest in money, some see it a means to enjoy life's experiences, and yet others think it is a tool with which to make people do want you want.

These various reasons are mostly ignored in the finance industry. A more recent theme has been the rise of behavioural economics and investing. This theory discusses the various foibles and biases we bring to our decision-making. It's a useful start, but it's not the whole story.

Again, the premise is that once you are given the 'facts' or made aware of your biases, you will automatically correct them and away you go. Having knowledge is one thing but putting that knowledge into practice is quite another.

We've found that our approach to investing reflects our personality.

In the book, we use a personality identifier called the 9 Types or the Enneagram Assessment to assist you in understanding individual personalities and the influence this plays in your approach to investing. Having our Investment Map that recognises your motivations, strengths and potential weaknesses can be very helpful, and even enlightening.

## Timeless investment principles

Along with our personalities, there appear to be certain principles that lie at the heart of many successful investment strategies. Many investors have their favourite set of investment principles and there's no shortage of them to choose from. Among the many, we have defined the eight key principles that we believe are applicable to all asset classes and will stand the test of time through the cycles.

We note here that there are many principles that are applicable to certain time periods (e.g. *the trend is your friend*) but are *not* timeless. What we want to show you is a strategy for all markets, that can work at any time.

Truly timeless.

## A timeless strategy for all markets

Out of all this investigation and refinement, we developed a strategy that you may wish to pursue. Our hope is that you can apply it yourself to become a successful investor. Investing is not that difficult. But we can say that after 20 years as guys who have been intently interested in all matters investing.

Our aim is to give you a strategy as a place to start and to open your mind to what is possible.

## From macro to micro...

We have found that many books follow the same structure. The author sets out the premise or the theory and then spends considerable time showing the evidence to support the theory. While this book is no different, we've looked to avoid quoting *too* many of the figures, academic papers and statistics to support the book's central theme. We've done this because while we could provide masses of statistical support for all the principles — and it does exist! — we would undermine the simple message of the book.

Remembering the broader principles (e.g. that the stock market ebbs and flows over time) is of greater assistance when thinking about investment decisions. In addition to this, we have not footnoted or referenced every single idea, quote, theory or individual piece of wisdom, instead we've listed the books that we have read and used at the end of the book.

Many of them make for fascinating reading, and not only for understanding markets but also in the study of human behaviour.

*We believe that anyone can be*
*a successful investor.*

What we hope to do is convince you that with an understanding of a few crucial concepts, you can gain a good understanding of how the stock market works, and more importantly, how to increase your wealth from investing in shares. We would also like to show that you don't need to rely on the views and expensive advice of 'experts' in order to achieve your investment goals.

Indeed, they can often be downright damaging for your investment health.

As with many of the professions, there's a language that one needs to understand. But where possible we've avoided using language that confuses and sends you scurrying to the dictionary. We could spend considerable time detailing all of the principles, language and techniques of stock market investing.

Instead, we'll show you that there are a few core elements that, if understood well, will lead you to successful investment results. But first, we would like to explain why you do not need an expert to manage your own finances adeptly.

## A word on writing style

We've tried to keep the language simple and have minimised the use of needless jargon.

A glossary of terms is provided at the back of the book, so take your time and work through the chapters at your own pace. We've kept plenty of white space and used simple examples because we believe that a successful investment strategy should be kept simple to be effective.

Sometimes we have repeated a point several times — this is deliberate because there are a number of prevailing myths about investing that need to be dismantled, so a few times we have hammered home the point.

The eight timeless principles we detail in the book all make perfect logical sense as standalone principles but it's when you bring them all together that their true power becomes apparent.

Let's get started!

**CHAPTER 2**

# HEY, WHERES MY YACHT?

## Where are the customers' yachts?

In 1955, Fred Schwed wrote a book called *Where Are the Customers' Yachts?* The title came from a story about a visitor to New York. After admiring the beautiful yachts that Wall Street advisors had bought with money earned from giving financial advice to customers, he asked, simply:

*'So where are all the customers' yachts?'*

Even after 80 years, it's an unfortunate reality that fund managers and stock market advisors often make more than their customers. Instead, we'd like to show you a way to get your own yacht. Whether through managed funds or superannuation, almost all of us are exposed to the stock market in some way.

While you don't need to become an expert in everything, there is considerable financial benefit in knowing something about the stock market and the financial sector.

*It helps to understand how it operates, why managed funds will not maximise your wealth, and why it is better for you to manage your own money.*

In this section, we would like to explain some of the ins and outs of managed funds.

*Then we will set out a low-risk, low-cost method
of managing your investments that requires only
a small amount of your time each year.*

People often spend more time on deciding where to holiday or
what car to buy than they do managing their money and investments. Remember we said that investing is simple, but not easy. It's
simple because there are only really a few timeless principles that
you need to follow.

The 'not easy' part is that you must set aside a modest amount
of time to dedicate to managing your investments and controlling
your emotions.

## FIGURE 2.1 – HOW MANAGED FUNDS OPERATE

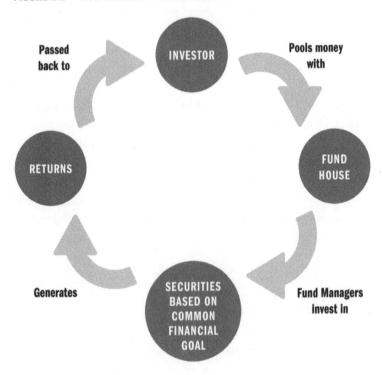

There are thousands of managed funds that you can choose to invest in, but most tend to work in roughly the same way, as depicted in the previous diagram. Your money is pooled and then invested along with other investors to the fund. Depending on the fund type, you will receive, in most cases, dividends and capital growth (when there is capital growth!).

Choosing the right fund can be a difficult process, but it usually starts with determining your risk profile. Determining your risk profile helps to narrow the range of investments that you would be comfortable investing in.

Your risk profile measures your appetite for risk. It runs along a continuum from conservative (investing cash in term deposits and government bonds with very little risk) to growth investor (investing in stocks and property) to aggressive investor (investing in high-risk areas like paintings, vintage cars, stamps and coins etc).

Once you have determined your risk profile — and because there are thousands of available funds — you can set about looking for the managed funds that match this profile. Thus, a 'growth' investor looks for managed funds that are deemed growth funds, and so on.

## Types of fund

There are essentially two popular types of funds.

### Index funds

Index funds aim to achieve performance returns broadly in line with a selected market index (e.g. the ASX top 200 or another such index). In these cases, the investment manager does very little active work or decision-making as the fund simply tracks the index. The fund manager makes no judgements about individual companies or future market movements. If the index in question returns 10% then the fund will most likely return approximately 10%.

### Specialist funds

Specialist funds are aimed at different types of investors. Some funds are more active than index funds. For example, these funds may select several 'growth' stocks and invest in them. These funds are designed to meet the needs of investors who are prepared for some greater risk and volatility in their investments.

There may be a technology fund that invests only in companies within the technology sector. While an index might return 10% in a year, the technology fund may return 5% or 25% depending on the results of the companies that are in the fund and the performance of the technology sector overall.

*In June 2012, there were 4,613 stock mutual funds in the US.*

*Consider that there were only about 6,500 publicly traded corporations of meaningful size in the US.*

*How do you suppose that if I don't have the intelligence to pick a good company out of 6,500 available, I can pick the right mutual fund out of 4,613?[1]*

## Fund fees

When it comes to investing money, many people seek advice from a financial advisor. This is not unusual, and a skilful financial advisor can add value to enhance your long-term wealth. However, in all cases, the advice they provide is not free.

Advisors can charge a flat annual fee or in some cases a percentage of your assets that they manage — for example, 1%. In most cases, these advisors will recommend that you place your money in a fund that also charges fees. Sometimes, therefore, you can be hit with two sets of fees — one from the advisor and one from the recommended fund.

There are various fees and charges when you invest in a managed fund, and funds don't all charge fees in the same way. For example, some charge entry fees, and others charge exit fees.

Usually, fees charged generally fall into one of several categories:

- fees when you move your money in or out of a fund, including contribution fees, withdrawal fees and termination fees
- management costs — fees for managing and administering your investments
- service fees — include advisor service fees, special request fees and switching fees
- fees to switch between one fund and another

Taxes are generally lower in a passive index fund. Active fund managers (who buy and sell a lot of stocks during the year) incur higher taxes due to the large number of transactions.

This, in turn, reduces the investment returns of the fund. The average managed mutual fund has an expense ratio of about 1%. That doesn't sound like much on the surface, but if it proves to be 1% of a 7% annual return, then it's a crippling drag on your ability to grow wealth because of the compounding effect foregone.

Over a 25-year period, an investor could hand over to the typical mutual fund with an average annual return of 7%, a shocking 30% of his or her income. The graphic in figure 2.2 shows some stylised fee scenarios.

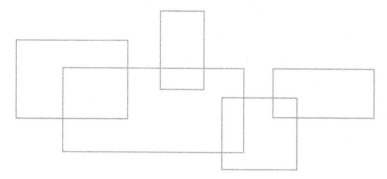

## FIGURE 2.2 – THE IMPACT OF FEES

| Manager | A (Passive) | B (Active) | C (Active) |
|---|---|---|---|
| Years invested | 10 | 10 | 10 |
| Start value | $100,000 | $100,000 | $100,000 |
| Index return | 7.5% | 7.5% | 7.5% |
| Outperformance | 0.00% | 2.00% | 0.00% |
| Fee | 0.15% | 0.90% | 0.90% |
| Net return | 7.35% | 8.60% | 6.60% |
| End Value | $203,245 | $228,191 | $189,484 |

- A — an index fund with no fees (you can do this yourself by purchasing what is called an ETF — explained below);
- B — a fund that is actively 'managed' by a financial advisory firm;
- C — an active fund that buys and sells according to the manager's skill.

Although fund B looks attractive, you need to remember that this outperformance has been delivered in a single year or period. In order to achieve these results over the long term, this outperformance would need to be achieved every year. As studies have shown time and time again, very few managers are able to outperform the index for any extended period and charge only a 0.90% fee.

> 'A recent study by Vanguard found that of 1,540 managed US equity funds in 1998, only 842 survived through 2012, or barely 55% of those in existence at the beginning of the period. In addition, only 275, or 18% of the total, both survived and outperformed their benchmarks.'
> JACK BOGLE[2]

## Compounding fees

Albert Einstein called compound interest the eighth wonder of the world. Financial advisors sometimes seem to think compound fees are the eighth wonder of the world. Alan Kohler of *InvestSMART* has consistently and tirelessly highlighted the conflicted fee structures of the industry.

Let's look at a stylised example, according to Kohler's premise and research.

For example, Kohler says, say you graduate and start with a $50,000 salary and have a couple of thousand dollars paid into your superannuation fund. The management fee might be 1% per annum, although by the time you add in transaction costs, insurance and taxes, it could easily be effectively much higher.

At 1% the management fee seems reasonable enough at $20 or so. Over the coming year you contribute about 10% of your salary, and hopefully you get some growth on your investment taking the super balance higher to about $8,000. The new fee leaps to $80, which is a four-fold increase.

Again, this might not seem too much, but consider what happens later as your balance grows.

*Obviously, this stylised escalation in fees is dramatic because the balance started from a low base.*

As your salary increases, so to do your contributions. And as the superannuation balance increases, you continue to get punishing increases in fees from the preceding year[3]. As Kohler has shown, the more you pay in fees, the less you get to keep[4].

What really hurts is not the fees themselves, but the compound growth which is not allowed to flourish as a result.

## Fund performance

There's no harm in paying fees if you can get 'value for money'. Higher fees should mean higher investment returns.

*Unfortunately, when managed funds are assessed in terms of investment returns, it shows that in aggregate managed funds, customers are not receiving value for money (fees).*

The performance of most managed funds is measured against what is known as a *benchmark*. A benchmark is simply a tool to compare how the fund performed over a certain time period. Thus a fund that invests in the Australian ASX index will likely benchmark itself against the index.

The stated objective of many funds is to either match or beat their benchmark. However, it is a sad reality that only approximately 10% beat the market or their chosen benchmark.

There are several reasons why investment managers will always have a difficult time beating the index. Chasing a benchmark index may be a mistake because:

1. The index contains no cash;
2. It has no life expectancy requirements — but you do;
3. It does not have to compensate for distributions to meet living requirements — but you do;
4. It requires you to take on excess risk (potential for loss) in order to obtain equivalent performance — this is fine on the way up, but not on the way down;
5. It has no taxes, costs or other expenses associated with it — but you do; and
6. It can substitute at no penalty — but you can't.

## Managed funds underperform

Typically, there are restrictions on investment managers and what they can do. All fund managers adhere to what is called a strategic asset allocation. This is where the manager is restricted to allocating a set dollar amount to each investment area.

For example, a 'growth' portfolio may have 50% in Australian funds, 25% in international funds, 5% in cash and 20% in government bonds. Such restrictions might mean the fund can't place 65% in international stocks (which might be a great opportunity when the Australian dollar is high) unless this is within the asset allocation range.

Even then, they will most likely stick to the benchmark allocation. The risk of underperformance should they choose to behave differently from other competitor funds could bring about severe repercussions for the fund manager.

Investment managers are also required to have a specific amount of the fund invested in the market. They're rarely allowed to 'sit in cash' if they personally think the market is overvalued. Imagine telling your immediate boss that you have placed 50% of the fund's $500 million in cash because you think the market is overvalued.

Great investors like Warren Buffett will do this, waiting for great opportunities — at the time of writing, he has a record US$128 billion in cash! But for many funds that will simply never happen; they'll simply always invest in the market. Therefore, any decline in the market — and periodically declines are inevitable — has a greater impact since you always have a large portion of funds in the market.

No wonder most funds never do much better than the index over time. Once you've deducted the fees, the odds are stacked heavily against such an outcome.

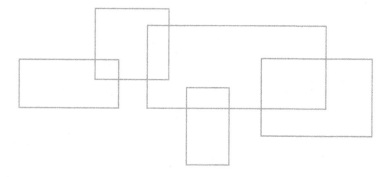

## FIGURE 2.3 – FUND UNDERPERFORMANCE

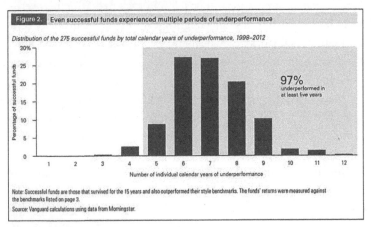

Source: Vanguard

## Paying for their own yachts?

Would you eat at a restaurant where the chefs didn't eat their own cooking? Or buy a Mercedes from a salesperson who drives a Lexus? You must ask yourself, then, why would you invest in a mutual fund where the managers don't put their own money alongside yours?

The first question you should ask any financial advisor who recommends managed funds, or an individual stock, is:

> *'How much of your own money do you have
> in the recommendation?'*

You may be surprised to find that funds managers are not all that keen on eating their own cooking. In the US, surveys found that close to half have stated that they had none of their own money in the fund they managed. About 60% of managers who managed foreign funds had no money in them. And about 70% of balanced fund managers had no money in them (this was particularly surprising since balanced funds are usually the most recommended to investors).

This misalignment does not feel too out of place when the recommended investment is performing well. Most people will not complain about fees when the stock market is rising.

But it's when the downturn inevitably comes that people begin to question what exactly they have been paying for.

*Unfortunately, the advisor's or fund manager's incentives are not necessarily aligned with yours.*

For fund managers, the name of the game is getting more funds to manage, which generates more fees, avoiding investments that other managers avoid so as not to 'run against the crowd' and, finally, ensuring there is a pay cheque at the end of every fortnight.

Below follows an old story.

There are two investors, one of whom is relatively new. He sees all the stock market traders clapping at the end of the day — a day when the stock market went down. He asked his more experienced counterpart why they were clapping given that the market went down.

The answer?

Because it doesn't matter to them personally whether they win or lose just so long as people are trading! Regardless of how the stock market performs, many managers are simply happy to receive funds to invest.

*'The number of managers showing no faith in their process is staggering. We can't think of why anyone should invest in a fund that its own manager doesn't invest in.'*
MORNINGSTAR (2014)

When it comes to managing money, many continue to believe that the experts can do a better job than we ourselves can do. There are myriad reasons put forward that convince you that it is better to have an expert looking after your financial future: money is complex, experts know better, you must be able to understand the economy, it takes a lot of time and energy, and so on.

However, once you understand the core principles of investing, it's *not* that hard, and not necessarily too time-consuming to manage your own finances. At the very least, we hope this book encourages you to think further about looking after your own finances and, importantly, planning your financial future. As you can see, the effort may prove to be well worth it.

**FIGURE 2.4 – INDEX FUND VERSUS MANAGED FUND**

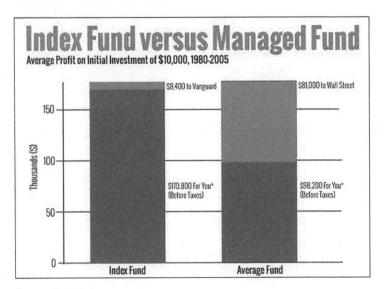

Source: Vanguard

If there's one key point that you should take out of this section of the book, it is that paying fees to financial advisors and allowing others to make decisions regarding your future will likely result in you failing to optimise your assets. And, ultimately, it will likely reduce your long-term returns from your investments.

Of course, that doesn't necessarily mean that you won't succeed or have enough money in the future. But by managing your own finances, you may well be able to retire earlier or simply enjoy more money to spend once you retire.

*In the next sections of the book, we will show you why and how you can invest your own money and avoid paying ongoing expensive fees.*

In fact, in the very next chapter, we will answer the question of why you should look to manage your own money.

# CHAPTER 3

# WHY YOU SHOULD MANAGE YOUR OWN MONEY

*'Unless you build a habit of making money on your own, standalone, you will find yourself, at some point, depending on the whims of someone else who will run your life when it's too late.'*
NASSIM NICHOLAS TALEB

## The 3 Cs

One flaw in most investment advice is that it is not sufficiently tailored to the individual. Most investment advice recommends the same approach for you as is delivered to other clients. This is based predominantly on your age, your risk profile or tolerance, and how much capital you have available to invest.

However, none of us are in precisely the same position regarding our finances or our stage in life, so it's sensible that we should have a personal Investment Map to guide us in our investing.

Here are three good reasons to manage your own investments, which we know as 'the 3 Cs'.

## Reason 1: Cost

When it comes to investing money, many people seek advice from a financial advisor. This is not unusual, and we do acknowledge that a skilful financial advisor can add value to enhance your long-term wealth. The cost of investing your money is best described as scaled, but asymmetrical.

*The more you invest,*
*the more you lose in fees.*

And the incentives are such that it is better for the manager to invest all your money rather than just some of it with a store of cash. Now if they add value that's fine — however, most fund managers underperform the wider market, and so you are paying fees to lose money (politely referred to as underperformance).

That does not make sense. Remember in many cases advisors will recommend that you place your money in a fund that also charges fees. And so, remember, you can be hit with two sets of fees — one from the advisor and one from the recommended fund.

There are various fees and charges when you invest in a managed fund, and funds don't all charge fees in the same way. Active fund managers (who buy and sell a lot of stocks during the year) incur higher taxes due to the large number of transactions, which in turn reduces the investment returns of the fund.

*Due to the opportunity cost — what might have*
*been achieved with that money instead — over*
*a long time period, an investor might lose a*
*shocking percentage of his or her*
*potential returns.*

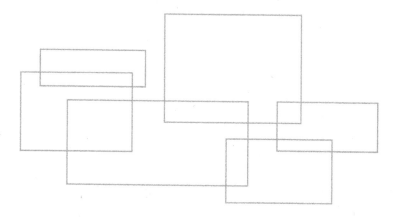

## Reason 2: Control

All funds have an established asset allocation. For example, a balanced fund might look something like the example below.

| | Asset allocation | Ranges |
|---|---|---|
| Cash | 13.2% | 0–25% |
| Fixed interest | 25.1% | 5–35% |
| Real estate | 8.2% | 0–20% |
| Equities* | 31.3% | 25–55% |
| Infrastructure | 15.2% | 0–20% |
| Commodities | 0.9% | 0–15% |
| Alternative assets | 6.0% | 0–25% |

*Equities might include a mix of Australian Shares, International Shares, and Private Equity.

Asset allocations incorporate a range of asset classes. One major drawback with these types of funds is that they are required to stay within the established ranges for the asset classes. So as above, cash can vary between 0% and 25%. However, if the market moves considerably, then the manager cannot go any higher than 25% cash.

This can be restrictive if you wish to, for example, increase your allocation to the market when it declines (so you can *buy low*) or reduce your allocation if you believe the market is overvalued (so you can *sell high*). Managing your own money allows you to move your asset allocation to levels that you consider appropriate.

As Taleb states above, you are at the behest of others if you don't control your own money.

## Reason 3: Choice

Managing your own money gives you greater choice in where to invest. For example, many funds and advisors have a home bias.

Although Australia represents only approximately 2% of global stock markets, people prefer to invest their money at 'home' in the Australian market.

*However, all markets ebb and flow, and sometimes it is prudent and more profitable to invest in overseas markets.*

Have a look at Figure 3.2, the 'quilt' of returns, which is a concept we'll consider a few times in this book. Notice how countries take turns at outperforming their counterparts. Also note how the average annual returns can comprise both years of enormous gains and enormous losses.

*If you spend some time looking back at history, the big gains very often follow immediately after the huge losses.*

If you buy when markets are down 50%, then your returns in the coming years are likely to be very good. Think carefully for a moment about this because it's a critical point! There's really no reason for holding a home bias! Instead, why not look to buy in markets that are cheap, and profit handsomely from the rebound?

Take some more time to look at Figure 3.2.

*Notice how markets that have experienced severe corrections often deliver strong outperformance over the years ahead, often within just 12 to 24 months of the preceding crash.*

Most markets work on very similar principles, and so it can be very prudent to spread your investments. There is no proven higher level of risk in overseas markets, and it is prudent to ensure that you have some investments overseas in order to reduce your risk. You'll notice that although a country's market might have an average return of, say, 8–10%, these averages can include years of huge gains and huge losses.

Of course, what we're interested in is participating in the huge gains (by buying *low*) and avoiding the big losses (by selling *high*). It's true that you can't time markets perfectly, but you can get close enough when you know what you're doing.

Think about the dramatic difference this could make to your returns. Especially because going from $100 to $50 represents a catastrophic portfolio loss of 50%...but going from $50 back to $100 is a gain of 100%!

## FIGURE 3.2 – INTERNATIONAL STOCK MARKET RETURNS

### International Stock Market Returns

| 2003 | 2004 | 2005 | 2006 | 2007 | 2008 | 2009 | 2010 | 2011 | 2012 | 2013 | 2014 | 2015 | 2016 | 2017 |
|---|---|---|---|---|---|---|---|---|---|---|---|---|---|---|
| SWE 66.1% | AUT 72.3% | CAN 28.5% | PRT 48.4% | FIN 50.1% | ISR -26.8% | NOR 88.6% | SWE 34.8% | IRL 14.3% | BEL 40.7% | FIN 48.0% | ISR 23.7% | DNK 24.4% | CAN 25.5% | AUT 59.0% |
| DEU 64.6% | NOR 54.5% | ISR 27.4% | ESP 50.2% | HKG 41.2% | CHE -29.1% | AUS 76.8% | DNK 31.1% | NZL 5.4% | DEU 32.1% | IRL 41.7% | NZL 8.2% | IRL 16.9% | NZL 19.3% | HKG 36.2% |
| ESP 59.2% | BEL 44.9% | ISR 25.7% | IRL 47.6% | ISR 40.5% | CHE -29.9% | SGP 74.0% | HKG 23.2% | DEU -2.5% | DNK 31.9% | DEU 22.6% | DNK 6.8% | BEL 13.0% | NOR 14.9% | ESP 35.6% |
| AUT 57.8% | IRE 43.1% | JPN 25.6% | SGP 46.7% | DEU 35.9% | ESP -40.1% | SWE 65.9% | SGP 22.2% | CHE -6.1% | SGP 21.0% | ESP 32.3% | BEL 5.1% | JPN 11.1% | AUS 11.9% | DNK 35.6% |
| NZL 57.6% | NZL 37.5% | DNK 25.3% | NOR 46.3% | NOR 32.4% | FRA -42.7% | HKG 60.2% | NOR 21.2% | NLD -9.1% | NLD 21.8% | NLD 31.8% | BEL 4.3% | JPN 9.9% | AUS 11.7% | NLD 32.7% |
| ISR 57.5% | SWE 37.3% | AUT 25.2% | SWE 44.6% | CAN 30.2% | EAFE -43.1% | BEL 58.6% | HKG 15.6% | BEL -10.0% | HKG 28.3% | BEL 28.8% | SGP 3.1% | AUT 3.9% | FRA 6.6% | FRA 29.3% |
| CAN 55.4% | ITA 34.0% | FIN 19.5% | DNK 29.8% | AUS 29.8% | CAN -45.2% | AUS 57.4% | AUS 14.7% | AUS -10.8% | AUT 27.0% | IRA 27.3% | IRL 2.6% | FIN 3.1% | IRL 5.3% | NOR 29.8% |
| AUS 51.4% | AUS 32.0% | AUS 17.5% | BEL 37.8% | SGP 28.4% | DEU -45.5% | ISR 54.6% | CHE 12.9% | ESP -11.2% | SWE 23.4% | CHE 27.6% | CAN 2.3% | ITA 2.0% | ITA 4.7% | DEU 29.6% |
| DNK 50.3% | DNK 31.0% | CHE 17.1% | AUT 37.1% | NZL 26.1% | AUT -47.3% | NZL 51.7% | FIN 11.8% | DEU -11.7% | FRA 22.0% | FIN 27.4% | FIN 0.6% | PRT 1.9% | ESP 3.5% | DEU 28.5% |
| NOR 50.0% | ESP 29.6% | DEU 15.0% | DEU 36.5% | PRT 24.8% | NLD -47.3% | ESP 45.1% | FIN 11.6% | EAFE -11.7% | AUS 22.3% | SWE 26.0% | CHE 0.7% | NLD 1.7% | JPN 2.7% | ESP 27.7% |
| PRT 44.3% | PRT 25.7% | FRA 14.4% | FRA 35.4% | ESP 24.7% | AUT -47.9% | AUT 44.1% | IRL 10.7% | CAN -12.3% | CHE 21.5% | CHE 25.9% | NLD -3.2% | CHE 1.2% | FRA 2.3% | EAFE 25.0% |
| IRL 43.8% | HKG 25.0% | EAFE 14.0% | ITA 34.1% | NLD 21.1% | GBR -48.3% | GBR 43.4% | DEU 9.3% | JPN -14.2% | ITA 21.2% | NLD 23.3% | AUS -3.2% | IRA 1.3% | SWE 2.3% | IRA 25.2% |
| FRA 41.0% | CAN 22.8% | AUT 12.5% | FRA 14.0% | FRA 20.5% | NLD -49.2% | NLD 42.0% | NZL 9.2% | FIN -15.1% | FIN 19.7% | ITA 21.3% | FIN -3.7% | EAFE -0.4% | EAFE 1.5% | IRA 24.4% |
| EAFE 39.2% | SGP 22.3% | FRA 10.6% | NLD 32.5% | EAFE 11.6% | ITA -49.2% | PRT 41.7% | GBR 8.8% | FIN -15.7% | EAFE 17.9% | GBR 20.7% | EAFE -4.4% | HKG -0.5% | SGP 1.5% | FIN 24.0% |
| ITA 39.0% | EAFE 20.7% | DEU 10.5% | FIN 31.0% | NZL 9.9% | SGP -50.0% | DEU 37.1% | FIN 8.2% | IRA -16.1% | FIN 16.5% | FRA -4.5% | EAFE -4.5% | NLD -1.3% | BEL 0.6% | CHE 23.6% |
| HKG 38.1% | ISR 20.3% | NLD 10.2% | GBR 30.7% | GBR 8.4% | HKG -51.2% | FRA 33.0% | ISR 5.0% | HKG -16.0% | GBR 15.3% | GBR 12.3% | EAFE -5.4% | SWE -4.0% | FIN -0.5% | FIN 21.9% |
| SGP 37.6% | GBR 19.6% | HKG 9.4% | ITA 30.4% | PRT 7.3% | PRT -51.8% | ISR 32.5% | NLD 2.2% | IRL -17.5% | NZL 13.5% | NZL 12.2% | GBR -6.6% | NZL -5.4% | FIN -3.3% | SWE 21.9% |
| BEL 30.9% | FRA 13.2% | SGP 7.4% | CHE 28.2% | CHE 6.1% | NZL -53.4% | ITA 30.0% | BEL 0.2% | GBR -17.9% | CAN 9.9% | ISR 11.9% | FRA -8.8% | GBR -7.5% | CHE -4.0% | AUS 20.2% |
| JPN 26.2% | DEU 16.7% | NZL 6.9% | EAFE 26.9% | ITA 2.7% | FIN -54.7% | CHE 26.6% | FRA -3.2% | PRT -21.9% | JPN 8.4% | IRL 11.1% | ITA -8.6% | AUS -9.8% | IRL -6.8% | IRL 19.8% |
| CHE 35.0% | JPN 16.0% | NZL 3.2% | CAN 18.4% | SWE 1.5% | NOR -63.9% | DEU 26.6% | PRT 10.5% | ITA -22.3% | IRL 6.3% | DEU -9.9% | DEU -14.2% | DEU -6.8% | BEL -18.5% | ITA 18.5% |
| GBR 32.1% | CHE 15.6% | ITA 3.1% | JPN 17.8% | BEL -1.9% | IRL -66.2% | IRL 12.9% | ITA -14.1% | ISR -27.6% | ESP 5.0% | PRT 6.4% | CAN 6.4% | CAN -21.2% | ESP -15.4% | CAN 16.9% |
| NLD 29.2% | NLD 13.3% | IRL -1.0% | JPN 6.3% | JPN -4.1% | AUT -68.2% | FIN 12.7% | IRL -17.7% | FIN -35.0% | ESP 6.7% | AUS 4.3% | AUT -29.4% | IRL -17.7% | SGP -15.2% | NZL 12.7% |
| FIN 20.5% | FIN 7.1% | ISR -2.1% | ISR -4.9% | IRL -19.6% | IRL -71.7% | FIN 6.4% | ISR 21.1% | AUT -36.0% | ESP -3.9% | ISR -17.3% | SGP -37.7% | PRT -23.6% | CAN -24.5% | ISR 2.6% |

| Abbr | Country - Index | Annual | Best | Worst |
|---|---|---|---|---|
| EAFE | MSCI EAFE Index | 8.60% | 32.46% | -43.06% |
| AUS | Australia - MSCI Australia Index | 11.99% | 76.8% | -50.0% |
| AUT | Austria - MSCI Austria Index | 7.50% | 72.30% | -64.22% |
| BEL | Belgium - MSCI Belgium Index | 8.57% | 58.59% | -66.15% |
| CAN | Canada - MSCI Canada Index | 10.82% | 97.4% | -45.2% |
| DNK | Denmark - MSCI Denmark Index | 13.62% | 58.25% | -47.33% |
| FIN | Finland - MSCI Finland Index | 6.37% | 50.0% | -54.47% |
| FRA | France - MSCI France Index | 8.77% | 41.0% | -43.7% |
| DEU | Germany - MSCI Germany Index | 11.47% | 64.8% | -45.5% |
| HKG | Hong Kong - MSCI Hong Kong Index | 12.40% | 60.2% | -51.2% |
| IRL | Ireland - MSCI Ireland Index | 2.42% | 47.56% | -71.72% |
| ISR | Israel - MSCI Israel Index | 7.79% | 57.54% | -28.84% |

| Abbr | Country - Index | Annual | Best | Worst |
|---|---|---|---|---|
| ITA | Italy - MSCI Italy Index | 4.05% | 39.0% | -49.2% |
| JPN | Japan - MSCI Japan Index | 7.16% | 36.2% | -29.1% |
| NLD | Netherlands - MSCI Netherlands Index | 9.67% | 43.0% | -47.9% |
| NZL | New Zealand - MSCI New Zealand Index | 11.02% | 57.76% | -53.03% |
| NOR | Norway - MSCI Norway Index | 11.57% | 88.61% | -63.91% |
| PRT | Portugal - MSCI Portugal Index | 2.99% | 48.37% | -51.78% |
| SGP | Singapore - MSCI Singapore Index | 11.59% | 74.00% | -47.34% |
| ESP | Spain - MSCI Spain Index | 8.75% | 59.2% | -40.1% |
| SWE | Sweden - MSCI Sweden Index | 12.96% | 66.1% | -49.2% |
| CHE | Switzerland - MSCI Switzerland Index | 10.35% | 35.0% | -25.9% |
| GBR | United Kingdom - MSCI United Kingdom Index | 7.14% | 43.4% | -48.3% |

Past performance does not guarantee future returns. The historical performance is meant to show changes in market trends across the top international stock markets in the MSCI EAFE ex. U.S. over the past fifteen years. Returns represent total annual returns (reinvestment of all distributions) in U.S. dollars and does not include fees and expenses. The investments you choose should reflect your financial goals and risk tolerance. For assistance, talk to a financial professional. All data are at 12/31/17.

Source: Novel Investor[1]

Take some time to think about this. The buy and hold investor can periodically see half of an investment wiped out. The patient investor holding some cash is free to wait and invest in markets when they are dirt cheap. The concept of 'average' returns can be deeply flawed.

With the advent of exchange-traded funds (ETFs), investing overseas is no longer prohibitively expensive. And it can increase your overall returns. Notice that seldom does one single market significantly outperform over the long term...or even the short term.

*In many cases, last year's loser becomes one of the following years' greatest winners.*

Yet in many cases, fund managers are reluctant to invest in 'losers' because they worry about what their investors or boss might say. It's often much easier for them simply to follow the crowd.

*All markets suffer periods of underperformance.*

With an appropriate asset allocation and rebalancing map, these periods of underperformance can be your advantage. How? By allowing you to take advantage of investment opportunities as they arise in overseas markets. And these opportunities come around regularly if you can look overseas as well as at home. It's fundamentally very simple: buy low, and you will achieve better results!

**CHAPTER 4**

# THE SOLUTION: A TIMELESS INVESTMENT PHILOSOPHY

## Stocks don't always go up...they cycle!

This is the longest — and in some respects the heaviest! — chapter of the book. If you find any of the information difficult to absorb at first then you can skip ahead to the next chapter and just remember this key point: *stock markets don't always go up*. Stock markets move in cycles. So the returns can either be amazing (if you buy when markets are cheap) or terrible (if you buy when they're expensive).

Much of this chapter is simply data and charts that prove and underscore this simple point. Our philosophy holds that we want you to invest in bull markets when the odds are in your favour. And we want you *not to* invest in bear markets, when you will lose money. To achieve this, then you do need to buy and sell investments.

You can't simply buy investments and blindly hold them come what may. The detail that follows in this chapter explains why this is the case. But that's all it's really saying.

## A strategy for all markets

A timeless investment strategy is one that works in all markets. Fads will always come and go. Sometimes buy-and-hold investing will become very popular, for example.

In other decades, it will drift back out of favour as secular bear markets take hold, and as investors lose faith in markets delivering positive returns over an acceptable timeframe. For example, the buy-and-hold approach would have delivered dramatically negative real returns in bear markets, such as between 1966 and 1982. It's fine in hindsight to say you'd have stayed the course and loaded up for the next cycle.

But in real-time, that wasn't what most average investors were doing through 17 years that might've torched nearly three-quarters of their purchasing power, before dividends. As you can gather from the chart below, at the time of writing, we're now almost inevitably heading into another period of below-average returns or worse in the US stock market.

**FIGURE 4.1 – REAL DOW JONES RETURNS, 1946 TO 2018**

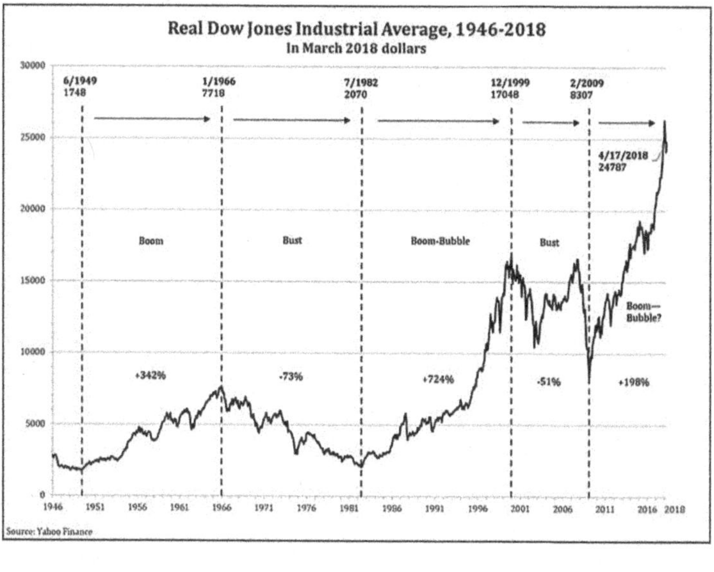

Now you might justifiably say that by not using a log scale, the above chart overstates the apparent inflation of the narrow Dow Jones index in the US. As such, the following chart of the full S&P

500 index in the US is dragged back to 1870 using a log scale and inflation-adjusted returns, which presents a more realistic picture.

**FIGURE 4.2 – INFLATION-ADJUSTED RETURNS, 1871 TO PRESENT**

Source: Advisor Perspectives

What this suggests is that long periods of significantly negative real returns have periodically been a feature of stock markets throughout modern history. In the US, these have included from 1906 to 1921 (–69%), or from 1929 to 1949 (–59%), in addition to 1966 to 1982.

Of course, in the real world, nobody buys all their portfolio at the market peak and then never invests again. And this doesn't mean there's no place for passive investing. But long-term buy-and-hold investors should remain under no illusions about how long markets can run against them for if they get their timing wrong.

What we're interested in is finding a better way that allows you to capitalise on the bull markets, and you can do this if you're prepared to look more broadly at global markets.

## Why a philosophy is important

In investing, it is critical to have a philosophy as well as a system based on a set of principles. Successful investors such as Warren Buffett and George Soros take a systematic approach to investing. In this book, we'll talk about the importance of personality, and the reason why it is critical to success.

If you invest your own money, but you have not developed a system or underlying philosophy, then you can only be investing based on emotion, gut feel, or instinct. While these attributes may be beneficial for some areas of your life, we certainly don't recommend them for investing!

> *Investing should be done with a strong emphasis on numbers, history and probabilities.*

In our experience, investing based on emotions doesn't lead to superior returns. Many investors invest this way and they fail to understand the importance of having a systematic approach. Equally, both of us have met people who believe the stock market is a complex beast requiring an in-depth knowledge of mathematics and finance. However, we don't believe this is the case.

Common sense and a cool head are really what's required. While we are both highly qualified in finance, there's very little to stop anyone from undertaking a successful investment career. The knowledge part of the market is easy to understand, and we mentor those interested in taking control of their own financial future.

## Our philosophy

There are three dominant aspects to an investment philosophy. We have developed ours from our combined decades of observing and investing in stock markets all over the world. But this philosophy can equally be applied to all investments regardless of whether they are in stocks, real estate, bonds, or even vintage cars.

*The first investment part of the investment philosophy is based on the adage: 'Don't lose money'.*

This sounds extremely sensible; however, most experienced investors will tell you it is the reward side of investing that gets most of the attention. Even in a low interest rate era, everyone wants to talk about where you can seemingly get high-reward investments. Put simply, you will fail more often in investing as a result of focusing too much on the rewards — that are *potential* rewards by the way — if the risks are routinely ignored.

For the past 20 years, we have sought an investment strategy that is low risk but provides an opportunity for high returns. It's probably fair to say that this is considered the 'holy grail' of investing. Of course, everyone wants low-risk investments that deliver high returns. However, that doesn't mean that a low-risk, high-reward portfolio is impossible to achieve.

## Risk: the traditional view

Before we tackle other issues, we should discuss the traditional view of risk, and why we believe it is not entirely appropriate for investors. By traditional, we mean the widely held view of risk, and that which is taught in business schools and finance degrees around the world.

Academic literature tends to define risk as *volatility*.

But the truth is volatility is not the same thing as risk. We've never heard anyone complain about volatility when the market is going up, after all! And, in fact, volatility can be your friend if it presents you with opportunities to buy low and sell high. The finance industry promotes the traditional view of risk along with the idea of buy-and-hold because of two reasons.

One reason is that the industry generally believes that buy-and-hold is the best approach for investors. Now, let us state for the record that we don't entirely disagree, but where we vary relates to cycles and market valuation. In discussions with many people, we find that most believe in a buy-and-hold approach through default.

We think this is because of what the mainstream finance and media industry promote.

*In short, most folks are told and taught to believe that you can't beat the market, and therefore you shouldn't try.*

Consider the long term, they say, *'you should just buy-and-hold (with a bit of tinkering) an index fund'*. Or alternatively, *'let a financial advisor in a team with a fund manager attempt to beat the market of your behalf'*. This view is based on the flawed assumption that no single investor knows anything more than anybody else and so the company stock price reflects all the available information at that point in time.

Thus, there isn't any opportunity to benefit from having information that could give you an advantage, they suggest. The much-advertised argument also states that in the long term, your portfolio will achieve a long-run return of approximately 8–10% average annual returns.

This is misleading on several levels, and we will show you exactly why this is the case later in the book.

## Buffett's view on risk

Opposing this traditional view are successful investors like Warren Buffett, who state that risk is really about a permanent loss of capital. We like this view. A stock price will fluctuate for many reasons, which will often have nothing at all to do with risk.

If you look at the companies in the ASX in Australia, most company stock prices change daily, but if you look closely, many simply follow what the US markets are doing. There will be variations and differences, but in general, the ASX follows the US market, especially when there is trouble in global markets. Notice how Australia was humming along nicely until the US decided to crash in 2008, and we as loyal followers (along with other countries) crashed along with it. After the crash, the buy-and-hold advocates then drag out the old chestnut that you don't lose money over the long term.

*While this might be technically correct, there is a key distinction to be drawn between not losing money and not actually making any money in real terms.*

Look at the chart in figure 4.3 below.

Notice the large differences in the returns over, say, 10 or 20 years. Depending on *when* you invest your money, over a 20-year period, your annual returns can either be fantastic (17%) or miserable (2%). Then you need to take away inflation at about 2.5% and add back dividends of about the same.

Any way you look at it, you would not be boasting to your friends about returns at the low end of this range.

Look below and you soon see that investing when the risk of low market returns was elevated, you indeed received very little. Now, bear in mind we have used the US stock market for the example below. But the main point we want to demonstrate here is that investing using a buy-and-hold strategy doesn't always work.

**FIGURE 4.3 – A SECULAR BEAR MARKET**

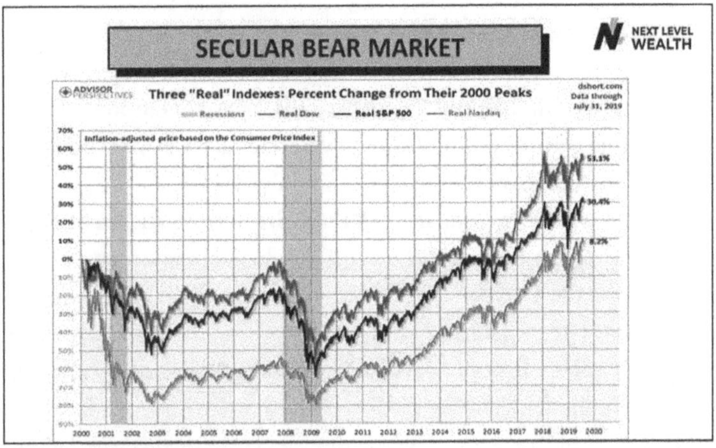

Source: Advisor Perspectives

## Our view on investing

Here is the main question you should ask every time you want to invest money. If I put my money in the bank and they offer me, say, 2% — with a 100% guarantee that I will get it back when I want — but I am being offered (and want) more than 2%, then what is the extra risk of losing money?

Therefore, we developed the *risk hierarchy* — which is a different way to think about risk and investing.

We will discuss the risk hierarchy only briefly because there's a full chapter on it later, but in short, you should think along the following lines. Cash is very safe but doesn't pay much in terms of reward (a small amount of interest). What cash gives you is a safety buffer, and *optionality*, being the ability to capitalise on great investment opportunities when they come around.

Bonds are also typically very safe and may pay a little more than cash. Stocks will generally do well over time, but there may be a greater risk of losing your money. Within stocks, there are relatively safer investments (diversified ETFs) and relatively riskier investments (such as some individual companies).

We will show you how you can apply our 8 timeless investment principles to minimise the risk of losses and enhance your returns in a low interest rate environment. Let's start by explaining further what we believe risk really relates to. We believe there are a few major elements to risk. We'll show you a solution to managing risk later in the chapter on the *risk hierarchy*.

## Risk: Your financial position and your personality

No one likes losing money, but risk varies according to our personal financial position. Losing $100,000 might completely change your life (as it did for many when the global financial crisis crushed their hopes when on the verge of retirement). But to a multi-millionaire, losing $100,000 will most likely not change their daily routine or their life's outlook too much. Our personalities play a major role in how we think about risk, which we discuss further below.

## Risk: Your level of knowledge regarding the stock market

Although investing successfully may be simple, the fact remains that the more you know about stock markets and their history, the greater the chance that you will succeed. We've seen many people who are investing in stock markets — either actively themselves or through their superannuation — who know very little about stock markets and their history. It's important that you understand the ebbs and flows of markets in order to generate solid investment returns.

## Risk: The overall market valuation

The stock market, like many things in life, goes through market cycles. In short, there are times when the stock market offers you above-average returns and times when it offers below-average returns. This is a result of the market cycles, and we'll show you how they affect returns when we discuss the principles of market cycles and mean reversion. Suffice to say here, there are times to be heavily invested and times to maintain a reduced exposure given the level of risk in the stock market.

So here is a different way to think about risk:

1. How long am I going to invest this money for? 10 weeks? 10 months? Or 10 years? This is important because stock prices change daily and depending on your timeframe, you should not get frightened by volatility (a word simply meaning the fluctuations in the stock price).

2. How much do I know about this investment? Are you knowledgeable enough to know what you are doing? For example, what is the price-earnings (P/E) ratio? We explain this ratio later in the book.

3. Are you investing systematically? Or are you investing or trading because you are bored? Or acting due to some other part of your personality?

**4.** Is the market valuation favourable? Is the market P/E cheap, average or expensive?

Let's think about the risk hierarchy as it applies to individual companies.

## Risk and individual stocks

Remember, every investor seeks the holy grail: an investment strategy that is low risk but delivers high returns.

After 20 years as an investor, Steve has said that successful investing is more about avoiding losses than it is in trying to find the next big winner.

> *The concept of risk relates to a permanent loss of your capital.*

Warren Buffett's first rule of investing is 'don't lose money', and the second rule is 'remember rule number one'. Investing is about outlaying money today with a plan to get more back in the future, however short or distant that future may be. When we speak of risk, we are really talking about possible future outcomes. Risk, in order to be useful in investing (or in most situations) must firstly have context to it.

In other words, it's a subjective proposition rather than an objective (numbers-based) one. Most investments are not a 50/50 proposition. Successful betting in horse racing, casino games, or poker, is about finding asymmetrical bets. Asymmetrical means there is a difference between the pay-off probabilities and the risk. A hand of four aces will see you bet heavily in poker, a pair of 3s … not so much.

That requires us to look and wait patiently for situations or investment opportunities that are asymmetrical. That is, there is plenty of upside if you are right but only a little downside if you are wrong.

Sam Zell, a US billionaire from real estate investing explains it like this:

*'Listen, business is easy.*
*If you've got a low downside and a big upside, you go do*
*it.*
*If you've got a big downside and a small upside, you run*
*away.*
**The only time you have to do any work is when you**
**have a big downside and a big upside'** SAM ZELL

Professional punters, poker players, or experienced investors look at the 'odds' (risk, based on the contextual probabilities) in relation to the potential pay-off before placing their bets. As Sam says, look for big upside with minimal downside.

So how do we manage risk?

Firstly, let's consider how the risk of buying the whole market is lower than when buying a single stock. If you immediately think 'well, yes, but the returns are lower', then we want you to go back to the start of this section — becoming wealthy over time is largely about not losing money! Remember most money managers under-perform the index.

Here's why:

## FIGURE 4.4 – TOTAL LIFETIME RETURNS FOR INDIVIDUAL STOCKS

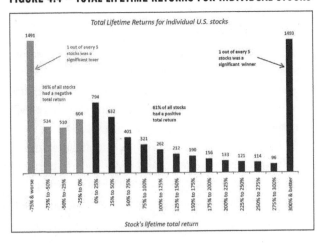

Here's the rub:

- About two out of every five stocks are a losing investment (39%).
- Nearly one out of every five of stocks lost at least 75% of their value (18.5%).
- 64% of stocks underperformed the Russell 3000 during their lifetime.
- A small minority significantly outperformed their peers.
- Fat tails — one out of five was a significant winner and loser.

To borrow a line from Dirty Harry:

*'Are you feeling lucky, punk? Well, are ya?'*

Index returns may be lower than returns from some individual companies but so is the risk! With an adequate time horizon, the lowest risk is probably achieved buying 'the whole market'. Thus, if we were to produce a risk hierachy for investing in stocks, it would look something like this — going from low risk to high risk:

1. Purchasing an all countries (global indexes) ETF.
2. Purchasing a single country index using ETFs.
3. Investing in a single sector/industry/style using ETFs.
4. Constructing a portfolio consisting of individual stocks.
5. A single company's stock.

This is not set in stone as there are so many permutations, but it at least provides some framework for assessing potential risk and returns. Therefore, Buffett says that if you don't know what you are doing, buy an index, due to the reduced risk.

By the way, here are the criteria if you want to be the next Warren Buffett:

1. Your name is Warren Buffett.
2. Start investing and thinking about money at age five.

3. Invest and do nothing else for 70 years.
4. Be born in the right place at the right time ...

We hope you get the idea. None of us is going to be the next Buffett! Thinking about buying individual stocks over a lifetime of investing means you are planning to select the best companies and investments more often than you lose. And those winners are going to perform brilliantly over the next 20, 30, or 40 years?

Best of luck! Our systematic approach shows that the returns you can generate from purchasing a single country's index or a single sector can be quite substantial. And the risk is much reduced from buying a portfolio of individual stocks. Have a look again at the quilt graphic back in figure 3.2 in the previous chapter.

Pay attention to the returns for each of the countries in the *best* years. They are impressive, to say the least ... even for countries that have delivered modest *average* returns!

And most are delivered when in the previous year they were among the most hated indexes.

### Remember ... buy low, sell high!

Our brains tend to absorb large volumes of information very well. Fortunately, there are only a few critical questions you need to think about when investing rather than ploughing through a company's last dozen annual reports. For starters, even asking yourself the most basic questions such as, 'Will this country go bankrupt?' is enough to give you a simple understanding of the level of risk (hint: they seldom do).

You can apply a similar methodology to sectors. Sectors of the economy, like countries, fall in and out of favour. But that does not make them inherently any safer or riskier simply because everyone loves, say, information technology this year, but not energy. You should gradually begin to see how important *reversion to the mean* is in investing.

Countries and sectors that have performed terribly in the recent past often go onto outperform in the immediate future. Of course, you are welcome to try and pick a single stock (or indeed pick a portfolio of 10 or 20) from the market of over 3,000, but you must understand the risk involved in investing in each one.

You can also aim to build wealth fast, but this usually means taking more risk — either by chasing longer odds or increasing the size of your bets.

*Big upside, big downside.*

As we get older, we often have less tolerance for loss-making investments.

Remember Buffett's golden rule #1: don't lose money!

Instead of seeing risk as a single event, you can look at risk as a hierarchy. You can develop our strategy that builds wealth steadily while adopting low-risk positions. This information alone is not the holy grail of investing … but it might help you get there.

Note: ETFs are exchange-traded funds that own assets, such as stocks.

They can be traded daily on the stock market, which often gives them good liquidity.

## Emotions and decision-making

Warren Buffett says:

> *'If you cannot control your emotions,*
> *you cannot control your money.'*

The second important component of our investment philosophy is understanding *you*. Recently there's been a surge in what is known as behavioural economics. It's different from the 'old' ways of thinking in that it attempts to take a more nuanced view of people's behaviour rather than simply pretending we're always 'rational'.

This is certainly an improvement on the old idea that people are completely rational (cold-blooded and objective) when it comes to money and investing.

One look at the history of stock markets and you can see that this is incorrect. However, even behavioural economics is not granular enough in order to develop an individual investment plan. When you understand someone's personality you can see where their beliefs about risk and beliefs about money come from. We believe and see that many people have different risk-tolerance or risk-aversion levels simply based upon their personality.

*Understanding yourself is critical is to avoid being overly emotional in your approach to investing.*

Hence, why we believe in taking a systematic approach. We seek to look at investments as rationally as possible based on our experience and knowledge, unlike many investors who make decisions largely based on how they 'feel' about the investment or what is happening in the markets. For example, just because the stock market declines, it does not mean that it has become riskier (which is the traditional view).

Understanding yourself is critical in developing an investment strategy and sticking to it when the pressure is on. Interestingly, this ties into our notions of risk. The first question a financial advisor often asks is: *'What is your risk level?'.* The first problem is most of us don't know.

Most folks end up saying: *'Um, about average, like everyone else?'* The second is that your risk tolerance will fluctuate with whatever is currently happening.

Why? Because when the stock market has fallen by 50% and the media are running a series of doomsday headlines, then you are unlikely to be thinking *'Wow, what a great time to put a lot of money into the stock market!'* (It usually is by the way!) We have watched people spending their money, and it often makes little logical sense. For example, we have a friend who is extremely risk-averse who sees the stock market as a gamble (he currently holds a few hundred thousand in cash earning next to nothing).

But he will happily spend $500 a week gambling on horse racing, football, and probably two flies racing up a wall! Logical? Hardly.

Steve:

*We could offer our friend an excellent conservative investment strategy that makes solid investment returns, but he won't budge because he is wedded to his beliefs, which stem from his innate personality and approach to money.*

*The reason why is that our individual personality heavily influences our approach to money — what money means and how it should be spent or invested.*

*My spending may not make sense to you, but that may be because we have a different personality type from each other.*

*Many things I do may not make sense to others unless they are of the same personality type. We have seen this constantly on several levels.*

> **There are certain personality types that are more interested in money even though their reasons may be different.**

Steve, being a Type 7 personality (freedom, adventurer, optimist) likes money because it gives him the freedom to do what he wants. No constraints or obligations that he doesn't like.

Pete, being a Type 5 personality (thinker, analyser, security-minded) has an interest in money because for him it's about gaining knowledge and some material security. Let us give you an example of how our individual personality can impact our investing.

Steve is a personality Type 7, so he likes excitement, and as a result, has a high-risk tolerance. Steve has come to understand that when the stock market is not very volatile, then he is prone to looking for some 'action'. Of course, this is most definitely not taking a systematic approach, and so he constantly tells himself to go and read a book, play guitar ... anything but looking for potential investments.

Why? Because our personality usually sees us repeating the same mistakes over time.

> *It's best to at the very least understand what our 'trigger' points are and acknowledge them and work on avoiding them.*

We recommend you look at the 9 Types in the appendix and understand what your personality type is. Select one of the statements and the corresponding number that resonates the most with you (if you can, try to avoid selecting two or more). It will give you some ideas about your own personal triggers and how to avoid them and how to avoid making mistakes when it comes to investing. We recommend using the 9 Types as a framework for understanding your risk level rather than more traditional approaches.

By having a systematic approach, we are seeking to minimise the role that our personality and subjectivity play in our investment strategy. We are all wise in hindsight because the emotions of the moment fade away and reveal that we should have acted when we hesitated (or vice versa).

> *Another reason why people don't invest correctly is that they don't have enough knowledge about how stock markets work and so are unsure what the right course of action is.*

As a result, personality takes over along with *groupthink* and people make mistakes by often following the crowd ... even when it is the last thing they should do. Another reason that we already touched on is the incorrect belief that 'buy-and-hold' works all the time. We will show you again later why it doesn't — it depends on what type of market you are in and when you buy.

Remember, the stock market comes to you and offers a range of returns at different times. When the market is cheap, you get great returns, but these are exactly the times that many investors withdraw their funds and become too scared to put money to work to get better than average returns.

This is partly because they don't have the knowledge about market cycles (discussed later) and thus allow their personality to dominate their decision-making.

It's important to understand your personality because when it comes to money and investing, people often make the wrong decisions at the wrong time. We seek to understand ourselves for the following reasons:

1. We get to understand our own emotions and see how they impact our stock market investments and our responses to market events;
2. We get to understand why we do the things we do with money as a result of understanding ourselves and what money means to us individually;
3. We get to control our emotional responses better and thus not make bad decisions by simply responding to events. We develop an ability to approach the market and our investments more rationally; and
4. We seek to counter our negative behaviour before we act.

## Steps in the decision-making process

Significant market events generally occur if there is similar thinking among large groups of people, and the news and media are essential vehicles for the spread of ideas. Indeed, news functions more often as an initiator of a chain of events that fundamentally changes the public's thinking about the market[1]. The media activity shapes public attention and categories of thought and creates the environment within which the speculative market events we see are played out[2].

In the crash of 1987, the US stock market fell 22% in one day. Robert Shiller set out to find why the market crashed. He discovered this: most investors started selling because the stock market started the fateful day by falling 200 points. Shiller then asked investors if they thought that economic fundamentals or investor psychology had been responsible. A full 60% stated that investor psychology was the reason.

Shiller wrote:

*'The crash apparently had nothing to do with any news story other than the crash itself, but rather the theories about other investors' reasons for selling and about their psychology.'*

So why were people selling? Because everyone else was selling! When it comes to making decisions, because we are part of a broader society, we are usually influenced in our decision-making by what others are doing and saying. Every asset class bubble, be it in property or stocks or another asset class, is a result of many people thinking and wanting the same thing.

*Unfortunately, it never ends well, and someone is always left holding the bag.*

People do not seem to perceive how often it's their own psychology, as part of a complex pattern of feedback that is driving the economy[3]. In the stock market, many investors do exactly the opposite of what they should do. Most do not actually sell when the market is high and buy when the market is slumping. The reason why is that at those times, folks are usually caught up with the crowd, their emotions, and the opinions of so-called experts.

*Ignoring historical facts and rational thought, emotions rule. People tend to make decisions by applying the least effort.*

This means we generally take the easy route first, and only after striking trouble do we tend to rethink and put some brainpower to work. What follows is an abbreviated version of how most of us usually make a decision. Most folks follow the crowd, and if that is the case, then you are probably not thinking straight.

One of our principles is to *buy low and sell high*, and we will explain why it pays to be a 'contrarian' investor. When it comes to something you don't know much about, like stocks and investing, people tend to undertake a predictable process:

1.  You read, see or hear about a company or the stock market in the general news media. Let's say it's a stock;
2.  Your friends explain how they just bought a stock because one of their friends or relatives is in the finance industry and he is rich (so he must know what he's talking about!);
3.  Perhaps you don't know much about stocks, but if your friend is buying, then it's probably a good idea. So you think about buying some;
4.  Your friend then tells you three months later the stock is up 50% and so you focus a little more on it by checking it out; and
5.  Your emotions take over because who doesn't want to make money the easy way? And so you buy some.

At this point, most folks have done little research, they know very little about what they are buying, and they don't know what they should be thinking about risk. They can only see the potential rewards. Most of us are happy to follow the crowd, and most of the time this is a sensible thing to do. Staying in a group is an evolutionary mechanism that is designed to keep us safe. We tend to make decisions using social proof, and so the stronger the belief (e.g. 'property prices never fall'), the more we are inclined to take on that general belief.

Swimming against the tide may seem like hard work, but it's profitable. The problem is the crowd often doesn't know what it's doing either! It is a bit shocking, but you will often find most investors know little about their investments (just think how much most people know about their superannuation). If you follow the crowd, then your investment returns will be the same as the crowd, and no better.

### *How we make investment decisions (being contrarian).*

Firstly, we avoid the crowd because we know that the crowd is unlikely to understand much about the investment and what the risks are. The most successful approach is to have a systematic method that delivers the best probability of you making successful investments based on sensible decisions. As John Templeton, a famous investor, said:

> *'It is impossible to produce superior performance unless you do something different from the majority.'*

It is difficult to stand alone, but we can tell you this is how you can get better than average investment returns in all markets. And with more practice, by using a systematic approach, your emotional framework will become familiar with the approach, so it gets easier over time. There are investors who do consistently beat the market.

Here's a brief summary of how they do it:

■ They have a system that they stick to and apply. This is usually based on being contrarian — that is, buying when the market is cheap. They don't wander off into the latest public fad or whatever is 'hot'.

- They don't follow the crowd (act emotionally) — you will often find that the most profitable investments are made when everyone else is running in the opposite direction.
- For example, we made a series of successful investments in 2009 when the global financial crisis struck.
- Again in 2011 buying US banks, in 2014 buying Russia (yes, Russia! We know what you may be thinking, but these are *very* successful investments that we still hold), and more recently after Brexit. On each of these occasions, investing appeared on the face of it to be a dangerous gamble.
- They follow market cycles and understand that there are times when it is better to buy and better to sell.
- Most of them use a rational decision-making approach when allocating their capital.
- They don't put all their allocated funds into the market at once. They 'average in' to an investment because they are aware that even cheap stocks and markets can get cheaper.

The proof is in the returns generated over a long period of time, and the superior performance of buying and selling shares using the value or contrarian method. The fundamental edge that value investors like Warren Buffett, George Soros and Ed Thorp use to beat the market is rooted in the psychology of individual investment behaviour, and this approach has been successful for the past 75 years.

Remember, though, if you don't know about yourself, then the stock market is an expensive place to find out!

## Time to be dynamic

*'History doesn't repeat but it does rhyme.'*

The final component of our investment philosophy relates to *time*. Following are a few concepts to think about regarding time and they are central to how you invest successfully.

**Static versus dynamic** — you must take what we call a dynamic view rather than a static view. The static view is the traditional approach and the one promoted by the finance industry: buy-and-hold.

We prefer taking a dynamic or active view rather than being static or passive. Now, this does not mean we must look or act every day. It means that we think dynamically rather than statically.

*We will show in our chapter on market cycles, that there are times to invest more and times to invest less.*

We know that over a full market cycle, the market offers different risks and rewards and so you need to think about timing and how it impacts your investments. We will explain further in the principle of market cycles and mean reversion why it is critical to use a dynamic approach and not a static one. The static approach states that the average annual return investors can expect is 8–10%.

This is somewhat misleading on two fronts and we discuss these further below.

## Average vs geometric returns

Now, let's deal with a finance industry furphy: *average returns*. This is important because it plays a critical role in investors thinking they will be OK in the long run. Firstly, average returns are compiled by adding up each year's returns and then dividing by the total.

For example, 1 + 6 + 8 + 9 = 24.

The average here is 6.

Now the average return from a stock market is taken from the starting point up to the current year. You often hear that the average return is about 8–10%. But the problem is that we each have a different starting point, and so our returns are bound to be different depending on our start and finish dates.

Incidentally, the 8–10% average annual return comes from a starting date of 1926! If you started then ... congratulations.

However, if you didn't start in 1926, then you are bound to have a different average return.

Notice in figure 4.5 that the annual average of about 8% seldom happens.

**FIGURE 4.5 – STATIC VERSUS DYNAMIC VIEW**

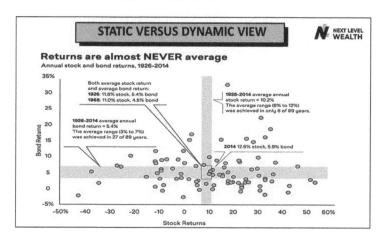

As an investor, you receive the geometric return, not the average return. Let's use the following example to explain why. From 1900–2019, the average annual return was 7.1% in the US market. You often hear statistics such as $1,000 invested in 1900 would be worth about $1.9 million.

However, the real figure is closer to $160,000, which is a geometric return of 4.7%. A big difference! This is because of something called the sequence of returns, which is explained below. Though the average gain was 7.1%, your actual real return was only 4.7%.

Geometric gains are the relevant ones because that is what you receive when the cash is deposited into your account. Another reason. The average seldom happens, and this impacts your returns. From 2000, a buy-and-hold portfolio's average return certainly didn't average 8–10%. In fact, it's closer to zero.

Why?

Firstly, if you invested at the top of 2000, you invested when a secular bear market (explained later) started, and so basically you made nothing. It's a little more deceptive still.

Firstly, average numbers are a result of addition.

Geometric returns are a result of multiplication.

Add the following and then get the average.

$1 + 6 + 8 + 9 = 24$.

Now the average is $24/4 = 6$. The *average* return is 6.

But the geometric return is what you get in stock markets because the gains (or losses) compound.

### That is why you seldom receive the average return.

The stock market effectively multiplies your gains (and losses), and so the average is largely irrelevant. The average is made up of totally separate individual returns. You are just one of the individuals that make up the overall average. Hence, you are not average!

You want to have a high geometric return because that is the actual amount you receive over your investment lifetime.

A simple example — you start with $100,000.

In the first year, you make 20%, and so your total capital is $120,000.

Great.

Now the next year, the market declines by 20%.

A shame, but no worries, because you still have your original $100,000. Or do you?

The average return is zero (plus 20%, minus 20%).

But the geometric return is negative, and you have lost 4% of your capital. How?

Because at $120,000 you lost 20% ($24,000), and so you ended up with $96,000. You lost $4,000! If you sell your portfolio you get back $96,000 (the result of the geometric return), not $100,000 (the average return).

Now obviously this is a deliberately simple example. But consider what might happen to your portfolio when the market falls 40%, 50% or 60%. Therefore, one of our timeless principles is *buy low, sell high*. You must buy *and* sell to maximise your returns.

**FIGURE 4.6 – S&P 500 RETURNS BY YEAR**

| Year | S&P 500 Return |
|------|----------------|
| 1999 | 19.53% |
| 2000 | -10.14% |
| 2001 | -13.04% |
| 2002 | -23.37% |
| 2003 | 26.38% |
| 2004 | 8.99% |
| 2005 | 3.00% |
| 2006 | 13.62% |
| 2007 | 3.53% |
| 2008 | -38.49% |
| 2009 | 23.45% |
| 2010 | 12.78% |
| 2011 | 0.00% |
| 2012 | 13.41% |
| 2013 | 29.60% |
| 2014 | 11.39% |
| 2015 | -0.73% |
| 2016 | 9.54% |
| 2017 | 19.42% |
| 2018 | -6.24% |
| Arithmetic Average | 5.13% |
| Standard Deviation | 17.08% |
| Geometric Average | 3.63% |

Remember what you get is the geometric return, not the average return. Still want to stay invested through the market declines?

Finally, another important part of our investment philosophy is understanding the role that the sequence of returns plays.

Put simply it can either bolster or cruel your returns.

It is also why we take an active approach and use another timeless principle of rebalancing to enhance our investment returns. Look at the chart below, which shows the personal wealth of two retirees, David and Carol. Note the only thing that has changed between the two investors is the order or sequence of the returns, while the average return in the same.

*Now look at the difference in final totals:*
*$2.5 million versus bankrupt!*

Therefore, you need to consider the sequence of returns in investing. It's prudent that after a good run, you rebalance your portfolio, and we'll show you how to do that later in the book.

**FIGURE 4.7 – THE SEQUENCE OF RETURNS**

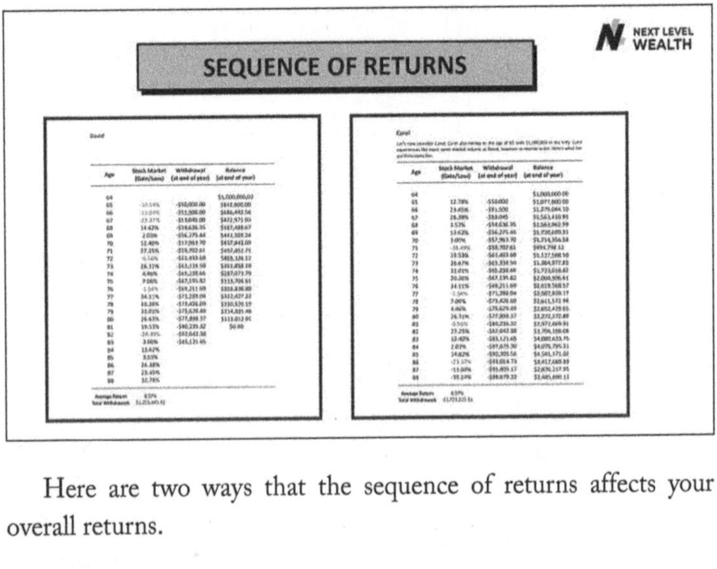

Here are two ways that the sequence of returns affects your overall returns.

### Negative numbers and compound returns

Make 20% then lose 20% and the average is zero. But you lose 4%. For a 20% loss, the required gain to get back to where you started is 25%. It's the same whether the positive or the negative occurs first. A 25% gain is wiped out by a 20% loss.

### Range of returns effect

As returns become more dispersed from the average, the compounded return declines. Three periods of 5% returns is greater than any other sequence that averages 5%.

6% + 5% + 4% = 5% average, but compound return is slightly lower at 4.997%.

As the variability of the returns increases (greater volatility), there is a decline in the beneficial effects of compounding returns.

The first year 9% + 5% + 1% = 5% average.

But the compounded return is 4.949%.

The bigger the swings in your portfolio, the more your compound returns may decline. This is most definitely what you don't want. Especially as you get closer to retirement. Therefore, the sequence of returns matter!

## How to buy low

Well done, you've made it through the heaviest chapter of the book! It's quite clear that staying invested through market declines can be severely detrimental to your financial health. Before we go on to the 8 timeless principles, let's have a brief look at a few real market cycles to give you some context.

# CHAPTER 5

# MARKET CYCLES

## Mastering the market cycle

*'The superior investor Is attentive to market cycles.'*
HOWARD MARKS, *MASTERING THE MARKET CYCLE*[1]

We all know that many things in life run in seasons and cycles. Each year has seasons, and even life itself has a cycle! It's the same in the stock markets and property markets as it is with most asset classes. There are fads and fashions, and sectors like information technology become 'hot' and gain momentum as investors and new money arrives.

Many of us are familiar with the typical cycle where a new idea gains currency and new money rushes in to take advantage of the opportunity to profit.

*A story develops of how the new product or service will change the world as the companies rush to the stock market to raise capital.*

Suddenly the public is talking about artificial intelligence, or self-driving cars, or robots taking all the jobs. Inevitably, the hot companies selling these products see their stock price rise as they become the new darlings of the market. As with most cycles, prices rise on the promise of future riches, and the stock prices of certain companies go through the roof.

Eventually, the products and companies fail to deliver the promised riches, and so the stock price falls back to earth. In stock markets, there will always be market cycles. At the broadest level, we have bull markets where valuations are rising, and bear markets where they are falling. Bear markets follow bull markets, and vice versa.

**FIGURE 5.1 – S&P HISTORICAL COMPOSITE**

Source: Advisor Perspectives

In figure 5.1, the bull markets are shown by the positive results, and the bear markets are shown by the negative results. Of course, in the stock market, you get dividend income too, and time periods are important for calculating annual returns.

In figure 5.2, you can see how the numbers play out with dividends included, and after taking account of time periods and inflation. As you can see, the returns from the market range from tremendously strong at 38.7% per annum to woeful at -41.2% per annum.

Hopefully by now an idea is beginning to click in your brain. When do the amazing returns happen? You got it — immediately after the awful returns.

When the market has been smashed, that's your cue to buy.

## FIGURE 5.2 – ANNUALISED RETURNS

| Year | Market Milestone | Percent Change | Number of Years | Annualized Return, No Dividends | Annualized Return with Dividends |
|---|---|---|---|---|---|
| 1877 | Low | - | - | - | - |
| 1906 | High | 421% | 29.3 | 5.1% | 10.1% |
| 1921 | Low | -69% | 14.9 | -7.5% | -2.0% |
| 1929 | High | 396% | 8.1 | 21.9% | 28.4% |
| 1932 | Low | -81% | 2.7 | -44.9% | -41.2% |
| 1937 | High | 266% | 4.7 | 32.1% | 38.7% |
| 1949 | Low | -54% | 12.3 | -6.2% | -0.8% |
| 1968 | High | 413% | 19.5 | 8.8% | 13.3% |
| 1982 | Low | -63% | 13.6 | -7.0% | -3.0% |
| 2000 | High | 666% | 18.1 | 11.9% | 15.3% |
| 2009 | Low | -59% | 8.5 | -9.8% | -8.1% |
| Now | - | 227% | 10.5 | N/A | N/A |

Based on inflation-adjusted S&P Composite monthly averages of daily closes.

We've used a chart of the US S&P 500 index above to make the point. But we want to stress that this pattern is far from unique to the US. Similar patterns tend to repeat over and over in mean-reverting markets, which national stock markets very often are.

Figure 5.3 lists out the bear markets in Australia since 1914.

They keep on coming as they always do. Cycles repeat.

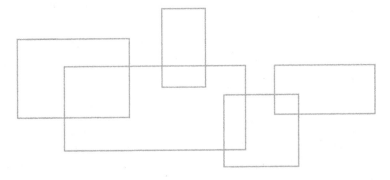

## FIGURE 5.3 – BEAR MARKETS IN AUSTRALIA

| Bear Markets in Aust shares | Mths | $ fall | % chge 12 mths after -20% | Recession Aust, US or both |
|---|---|---|---|---|
| Jun 14 - Dec 16 | 30 | -22 | -11 | YES |
| Jul 29 - Aug 31 | 23 | -46 | -30 | YES |
| Mar 37 - Apr 42 | 61 | -32 | 7 | YES |
| May 51 - Dec 52 | 19 | -34 | -13 | NO |
| Sep 60 - Nov 60 | 2 | -23 | 5 | YES |
| Feb 64 - Jun 65 | 16 | -20 | 8 | NO |
| Jan 70 - Nov 71 | 22 | -39 | -3 | YES |
| Jan 73 - Sep 74 | 20 | -59 | -38 | YES |
| Aug 76 - Nov 76 | 3 | -23 | 8 | NO |
| Nov 80 - Jul 82 | 20 | -41 | -13 | YES |
| Sep 87- Nov 87 | 2 | -50 | 3 | NO |
| Aug 89 - Jan 91 | 17 | -32 | 10 | YES |
| Aug 91 - Nov 92 | 15 | -20 | 54 | NO |
| Feb 94 - Feb 95 | 12 | -22 | 16 | NO |
| Mar 02 - Mar 03 | 12 | -22 | 24 | YES |
| Nov 07 - Mar 09 | 16 | -55 | -38 | YES |
| Apr 11 - Sep 11 | 5 | -22 | 10 | NO |
| Apr 15 - Feb 16 | 10 | -20 | 19 | NO |
| **Avg from 1900** | **17** | **-32** | **NA** | **NA** |
| **Avg Gummy Bear** | **15** | **-26** | **15** | **NA** |
| **Avg Grizzly Bear** | **20** | **-46** | **-23** | **NA** |

Based on the All Ords, excepting the ASX 200 for 2015-16. I have defined a bear market as a 20% or greater fall in shares that is not fully reversed within 12 months. Source: Global Financial Data, Bloomberg, AMP Capital

When you look at such charts and tables, it becomes easier to see how the cycles operate and obvious that there are times when it is better to invest a lot of money and times when it is prudent to invest less money (or have a different strategy). It's far easier to see the cycles with the benefit of hindsight, of course. Cycles are not always so easy to see in real-time.

Here are three key takeaways, then:

1. There are two types of bull and bear markets — secular (meaning long-term) and cyclical. Cyclical markets can be tough to negotiate as you come to believe you are in a secular bull market rather than a cyclical one. For example, after losing 50% from 2000 to 2003, the US market nearly doubled from 2003–2007, but it was a cyclical bull market rather than a secular one;

2. As you can see, secular bull markets deliver wonderful returns. Simply by buying at the right time, your investments will benefit greatly. In a bull market, you can just hoist the sail and let the market carry you along to great returns. When you start investing is much more important than what you invest in. Therefore, we use market cycle indicators such as the Cyclically Adjusted Price Earnings (CAPE) ratio — discussed in the next chapter — to help determine our asset allocation, and to assist us to adjust our allocations throughout the whole market cycle; and

3. Bull markets generally last longer than bear markets and are a much more pleasant ride.

Bear markets, depending on the levels reached in the preceding bull market, are usually shorter, but tend to have a bumpier ride that often ends with considerable losses. For example, from 1982 to 2000, the annual return was approximately 16%, or 666% in total.

*However, from 2000 to 2009,*
*you lost 59% in real terms.*

Now remember, that's 59% of the 666% gained (in effect, approximately 400%). Over the 1982 to 2009 period, your return was greatly diminished if your belief was 'buy-and-hold'. If you ignored market cycles, you would have made very little in 19 years in real terms. Such is the damage from ignoring market cycles and always adhering to a buy-and-hold philosophy.

## Ignoring market cycles

*'OK, I get it, the market cycles!'* you might say. *'But I'm happy with an annual return of about 8%'* (which, you are told, is the average return you can expect over time).

Here are some important points you may want to consider.

This figure is bandied about as the average expected return that investors should expect or aim for when investing over the long term. But as we showed, it is crucial to understand where you are starting out and how important this is.

If you were an American who had the misfortune to start investing in 2000, then your average real return was close to zero for a very long time (although if you were investing regularly then you'd have bought during the dips too). Yes, you might argue dividends — and we could counter with inflation — either way, it is nowhere near the 8–10% touted as the long-term return.

> *The 8–10% average return can be a very misleading number, depending upon how and when you invest.*

The reason why is because we know that averages as calculated by the finance industry don't always apply to you. The average of anything is the adding up of single entities.

6 + 6 + 6 = 18, with the average being 6. However, 9 + 5 + 4 = 18 too, and the average is still 6. Now if I said, well because of market cycles, your parents got the 9 + 5 part and you got the 4, then the average of 6 does not apply and it is misleading!

This simple example highlights the problems with each individual investor thinking they are going to receive an average return over the long term. The average is made up of some investors, like Warren Buffett, having above-average returns and many having below-average returns. Warren Buffett — like Howard Marks and other great investors — understand that investing at any point in time will not necessarily deliver long-term average returns to any single individual.

There's another issue regarding the long-term average. Investing works via multiplication not addition, and so the return you really want to pay attention to is the geometric return, not the average return. Remember our simple demonstration:

You buy at $1.

The stock moves to $1.20 for a 20% increase.

Now a corresponding 20% decrease sees you not back at $1, but at 96 cents ($1.20 less 20%, which is a drop of 24 cents).

And that is what you receive even though the average is zero (plus 20%, minus 20%, divided by 2).

> *Therefore, in many cases, investors receive a smaller return than the 8–10% you so often hear about.*

Another point worth underscoring again is that the market seldom returns the average in any one year. The ASX has delivered approximately average returns in roughly only 10 out of 89 years. This may not be a problem, but we know that bull markets generally have higher above-average returns, and bear markets deliver the opposite. The range of returns is also critical.

Because you get *geometric* returns, you need to pay close attention to the range and the sequence of returns. If your return jumps about from year to year, then the compounded or geometric return declines.

Again, a simple example should suffice. Three periods of 5%, then 5%, then 5%...averages 5%.

However, if you instead receive annual returns of 9%, then 5%, then 1%, then your geometric returns shrink, just slightly, to 4.949%. Again, not too bad, but if you throw in a negative annual return, say −15%, then you can see that your overall return is reduced even further, and you get further away from the much-repeated 8–10%.

Finance industry types tend to ignore or gloss over these issues because it's not in their interest to highlight these points.

The reality is that markets cycle, and these cycles can impact you greatly in investing.

*The average can be very misleading in terms of what the individual investor might receive as a return.*

## Capital gains and earnings yields

Most finance industry people (and the media) constantly talk about the overall level of the stock market rather than simply saying at a certain level the market is delivering a 2% annual dividend yield. Perversely, as the price of the market rises, the yield shrinks.

As Howard Marks is fond of saying, most folks forget that as the market rises so does the risk. But these days, most investors and the finance industry focus on the capital gains and forget about the market cycle. Because of market cycles, where the overall stock market gets 'expensive', there's an increased risk of losing a large portion of your capital. Where you should consider focusing your attention is not just on the potential for capital gains but also on the earnings yield.

Investors and the finance industry these days focus on the capital gains aspect of the market, instead of saying the market currently yields, say, 2% (or perhaps 4% in Australia). They rarely discuss the overall market level and how much further the cycle may have to run.

*What's seldom discussed is where we are in terms of the market cycle.*

Now I hear you saying, 'Well, yes, but that's better than 1% that we can get from bonds or cash'. And we agree — investing in a low-return environment is not that much fun, and consequently, you must get your money to work a little harder. But if you understand market cycles, you know that there will be better times to invest heavily. And while you may not be able to predict exactly when, what market cycles can tell you is that when markets are historically expensive, there's a large probability of losing some or a lot of your capital gains.

*That is why we advocate taking
an active approach.*

Capital losses can set you back because even if you are generating a 2–4% yield, then a 20% loss in capital value means you must climb much higher to get back to your starting point. You may know of someone who was planning to retire at the end of 2008 and was busy thinking about how to spend their million or so in retirement … only to find the global financial crisis wiped out a considerable portion of their wealth.

Note that single year's large negative return would not have shifted their long-term *average* return all that much. Averages can be deceiving, and it pays to be on guard.

## Summary of market cycles

Each stock market has its own cycle. And although global stock markets have increasingly moved in sync since the 1980s, there are sound reasons why investing on a global basis can be very positive to your portfolio. We will discuss the principle of mean reversion in the next chapter and show you a simple macro valuation indicator that can be used to determine which markets offer good future returns and those that should be avoided.

*Another important principle we use
is rebalancing.*

We will discuss rebalancing and how to use it in concert with the other principles to help deliver solid returns in low return environments and build your investment returns over the long term.

It's important to understand market cycles, the variations of those returns and importantly how to rebalance in order to get the most out of them. One often-heard complaint of the finance industry is that you cannot pick the top or the bottom of markets and so it's useless to try. Howard Marks' book has the subtitle of *Getting the Odds on Your Side.*

The quote at the beginning of this chapter does not promise to show you that you can pick the top or the bottom perfectly. But there's no need to either because when we invest, we don't invest at any single point in time. If you understand that stock markets and other asset markets cycle — and you have indicators that can alert you to markets being expensive or cheap (coming later in the book!) — then the probability of success is higher through actively managing your investments over the complete cycle.

There always have been, and always will be, cycles.

*If you have market cycles at the front of your mind when investing, you will understand that cheap markets offer higher long-term returns, and expensive markets offer low expected returns.*

Hopefully, you can now see the importance of understanding both the concept of bull and bear markets, and see the importance in understanding what type of market you are investing in. For each investment you make, where you start plays a hugely important role in where you finish.

In the coming chapters, we will show you a simple indicator that is very useful in gauging where we are in the stock market cycle, and what the expected returns will be.

## CHAPTER 6

# APPLYING
# THE 8 TIMELESS
# INVESTMENT PRINCIPLES

## The 8 Timeless Principles

Developed and honed over time by Steve, here are the 8 timeless investment principles that you can apply at any time, in any markets, to any asset class:

### 4 thought principles

**(i) Systematic investing** — if you don't have a systematic approach to investing, then on a long enough timeline eventually something will not go as planned and you will fail. Plan accordingly;

**(ii) Personality** — there are nine different personality types, and we all have our own motivations, strengths and weaknesses. Understanding your personality type and dominant beliefs will help you to invest with less emotion and more rationally;

**(iii) Market cycles/mean reversion** — market sentiment swings higher and lower over time, but over time valuations have tended to revert to an average or mean level; and

**(iv) Risk hierarchy** — some investments (e.g. individual companies) may entail a greater risk of permanent loss of capital than others (e.g. an all-World ETF that holds more than 1,500 stocks).

*Four action principles*

**(v) Asset allocation** — consider investments in uncorrelated assets. For example, cash and stocks are uncorrelated, so you might split your capital between these assets;

**(vi) Buy low, sell high** — exactly what it says on the tin! Buying low and selling high is a timeless strategy for all markets and all asset classes;

**(vii) Diversification** — there are several ways to diversify, including across multiple investments, by investing in products that are themselves diversified, and across time by carefully staging your entry to investments; and

**(viii) Rebalancing** — a critical part of any investor's armoury, to ensure that you are never over-exposed to any single investment position. Rebalancing helps to manage your risk and can improve your returns over time.

## Applying the principles

The principles are simple, and very logical. As standalone principles, they each individually make perfect logical sense. But the true power of the 8 timeless principles is how they interact together in harmony. When you pull them all together what you have is an investment strategy that can deliver the holy grail of investing.

> *That is, higher than average returns with lower than average risk.*

## The 8 timeless principles in practice

One of the difficulties with investment books is they often seek to cover every aspect of the stock market and many get lost in explaining the minutiae of investment language and details. That's not our approach or intention here.

We believe these principles form a holistic approach to investing, without missing the essence of good investing. We're keen to ensure you can distinguish between the signal (good times to invest) and the noise (daily media commentary and soundbites). Most days the stock market throws up noise, which is duly reported by a business media desperate for your clicks.

*Most of the day-to-day happenings in stock markets are noise that have no actual relevance to you as an investor ... but that doesn't mean it's **all** noise.*

Eventually, the noise becomes a signal, and that is when you can utilise the principles here to develop your investment knowledge. The principles here are what we call *evidence-based*.

After 20 years as private investors, and after reading hundreds of investment books, thousands of articles, academic papers, and the general media, these same principles have recurred throughout our development as investors. We also use the principles when we ourselves invest.

*These principles can also be used in any asset class.*

Buying an investment property? Well, you can use these principles to determine whether an attractive investment opportunity exists. Each of these principles stands on their own merit; however, as noted the most powerful benefits come from combining them.

We use the principles to develop a systematic approach, which ensures that you stay on the right track and avoid becoming tempted to drift. The idea is to use the four thought principles (systematic investing, market cycles, personality, and the risk hierarchy) to think about investments *before* you invest.

This ensures that you have stuck to the process and avoid making decisions based on emotions. The four action principles are there to guide you through the actual investment process when it becomes time to act. They show you how much to allocate (asset allocation) considering the macro valuation and market cycles.

We then discuss diversification raising issues you will need to consider in relation to your overall portfolio. We show you how to buy low and sell high to ensure you don't become too greedy at the top and too fearful at the bottom. And finally, we demonstrate the importance of rebalancing your portfolio and show you how important it is in contributing to managing your risk and ensuring your investment success.

The broad goal is to have you develop a rigorous systematic approach to investing. We're confident that combining a philosophy of investing with both the thought and action principles will enhance your stock market success.

## Let's get into it ...

Now you have an understanding of why the 8 timeless principles are so important.

Individually, remember, each of the 8 timeless principles makes logical sense.

*But the true power of this strategy will become apparent when you apply all 8 of the principles together.*

Why? Because the strategy has the potential to deliver high returns but with low risk.

Now that's a powerful combination!

Right, let's get stuck into it ...

# CHAPTER 7

# PRINCIPLE #1: SYSTEMATIC INVESTING

## 'Gotta have a system ...'

Successful people tend to exhibit successful habits. As the British comedian Harry Hill always used to quip:

*'You've got to have a system, don't you?'*

Having a system is important because it guides you to follow successful habits, until eventually, you make successful decisions intuitively. Too often people start out in business or investing without systems, and this leaves them exposed to mistakes and errors. There's an old rule of engineering that says if something can go wrong it eventually will.

The same line of thought can be applied to your investment strategy. As such, you need a system to protect yourself in all markets. A consistent routine of good habits will set you up in the best possible stead for a successful life, and investing is no different.

## Staying in your lane

Have you ever been stuck in traffic and then decided to change lane to try to get ahead? Yep, same here! And did it work? Well, sometimes it does.

But just as often the lane you ducked out of suddenly sees the traffic start to move ... at least in part because of the people doing just what you did! And then, of course, the lane you moved into starts to crawl.

*Instead of chasing the latest fad, as an investor what you need is a systematic approach.*

And then you need to stick to that system. Quite often the investments with the best prospects are those that have underperformed recently. And the opposite holds true as well. You shouldn't be tempted to abandon your strategy in the quest to chase short-term returns. Patience will pay off in the end if you stick to your system.

## Systematic investing: it's the process that counts

Many people are content to leave the management — and outcomes — of their investments to others. However, we believe it's important to have some type of understanding of finances and investing system if you intend to be in any way active in the management of your investments (which we think you should be).

Think about this statement:

*'I always decide to buy and sell my stocks by gut feeling because I think my emotional state is critical to my success as an investor.'*

If you don't agree with this statement, then you must have a system of some sort. If you don't have a system, on the other hand, then we're afraid to tell you, this is effectively the way you invest! Buffett's sidekick Charlie Munger says that although investing is simple it is not easy, and if you think it is, then you are stupid (no offence intended, we're sure!). Having a system can make help to make you less stupid in the markets.

Buffett is on record as saying they employ four filters (yes, there's a book on them) when it comes to deciding where to allocate

Berkshire's capital. In other words, Buffett does not let emotions, vibe, feelings, or gut instincts play any part in his approach.

Nor should you.

Older experienced investors can sometimes appear to make predictions based on their gut feelings. But the reality is that they are simply basing their opinion on a lifetime of experience and historical knowledge.

*As they say, history doesn't repeat, but it rhymes.*

Systematic investing is where you have developed a rational process that contains ground rules and signals for buying and selling stocks. Systematic investing is important because its primary aim is to assist you in your decision-making process. That is, avoid using your gut instincts.

Steve says he can pick an inexperienced investor from an experienced one simply by determining whether they have a system. Most inexperienced investors buy and sell based upon hunches. Yes, they'll make money sometimes, but usually, they lose or underperform overall because they let emotions such as greed and fear dominate their decision-making.

## What is systematic investing?

Success in investing over time is more about process than outcome. A good process will not mean all your investments are winners. After all, every investment involves a mixture of skill and luck. You can control your skill or your process, but you can't control luck. Sometimes you will be blessed with luck, and other times cursed. But as Gary Player, the champion golfer said:

*'The more I practise, the luckier I get.'*

What you are doing when you develop a systematic approach, is training yourself to ignore your subjective and emotional approaches to making decisions. Having a system does not insulate you from emotions that come into play with investing. Even experienced investors get that initial onset of panic when your stock drops 20% in a day on an unfavourable earnings announcement.

Now allow us to contradict ourselves a little. Systematic investing is both easy and difficult. The 'difficult' part comes first. It's in the development process. You develop your system and then sit back and implement it. But you suddenly have doubts when you see your most recent purchase declines another 10% or 20%.

Yikes! *My system must be wrong!*

Or, just as bad, you sell a stock and watch it climb 20% higher after you sold it. Suddenly there is an overwhelming urge, a temptation to fiddle, tweak or adjust your system because you didn't capture that last 20% rise or avoid that initial 20% fall.

> **There are very few investors who calmly say:**
> **'Oh yes, it climbed another 50%, but I'm OK**
> **with that. My system told me to sell,**
> **so I followed the rules.'**

Now simply announcing to the world that you have developed a set of buy and sell rules does not make you a systematic investor. But *sticking to it* does! When you find yourself itching to buy or sell an investment, go back to your system. Does it comply? Or are you making your decision based on a fear or greed type basis?

Are other investors influencing you?

There are many trite slogans when it comes to investing. Twitter, like Facebook, is full of preachers with pithy aphorisms such as: *'Sell your losers, and let your winners run'*. Of course, no one tells you how long you let your winners run for. Or what happens if it starts trending downwards? How long do you let it decline before you determine it's a good time to sell?

Steve said he watches in amazement how people become interested in a company once it has run up 50% but didn't want to know about it when it was down 50%. Or alternatively, change their mind regarding an investment because it declines 50%. Steve calls it 'emotional price discovery'. By the way, we see these same dynamics in the property market!

## Developing a systematic approach

There are many ways to make money in the stock market. Ignore those who tell you that their method is the *only* way to make money in the stock market. What's important is having a systematic approach to buying and selling stocks.

### *Firstly, read … widely!*

Read investments books about technical analysis, value investing, growth investing, and others. You will find that eventually you naturally gravitate toward a style that suits you. You may be time-constrained, so day trading is not for you. You may determine that you want to use technical analysis (reading chart patterns) as part of your approach. You may prefer a style like value investing or looking for young companies that can experience rapid growth.

In the development phase, you can revise your system, but do so based upon your reading, not by what is happening in the stock market that day.

Secondly — talk to other investors. Ask them how they approach it. Do they have a system? Does it sound like a methodical approach or just haphazard? Are they experienced (and, no, Bitcoin experience doesn't count!)? Don't count them out just because they didn't beat the market last month or year. No system works perfectly 100% of the time — what you need is a system that will deliver above-average returns *over time*.

Finally, a word of caution.

*Developing a repeatable system takes time.*

You will likely go through phases where you favour one approach over another, especially when your 'system' appears to be not working. Nothing makes you question your system like having a bad run. It's amazing how suddenly you think technical analysis or fundamental investing could be the answer. If you think deeply about your approach and develop your own system, then investing will become easier because you will not be ruled by emotions.

## Actioning a systematic approach

It's really all about the process. If you have a flawed process, then you are simply bound to repeat your mistakes. You would be surprised though to understand that it is usually the last thing we choose to inspect when a decision 'goes against us'. It is natural to look externally for blame rather than internally.

And in some cases, it will be an external issue, that results are a failure, not your internal process. But if the process is right, then you will win more than you lose.

People are patterns. The principles are timeless in their application to investing.

The remaining seven principles that follow will now help you to develop your systematic approach.

# CHAPTER 8

# PRINCIPLE #2: PERSONALITY/DECISION-MAKING

## Personality matters

In life, we all tend to think we're unique. And in one sense that is true. But, on the other hand, we're probably more like others than we care to admit.

In our Next Level Wealth coaching programs, we've found that we see the same few personality types repeatedly. This is not entirely coincidental, since broadly there are three main personality types that are in some way motivated by money and wealth.

These personality types are the achievers (motivated by significance), thinker/analysers (motivated by security), and adventurers (motivated by freedom).

### Why study your personality type?

Why is it important to consider your personality at all? Because once you understand your motivations, strengths and weaknesses, you can recognise and understand your behaviour patterns and become a more rational investor.

At Next Level Wealth we have developed a personality test and an Investment Map that can be followed by each personality type.

Take the test in the appendix at the back of the book.

You can then email us to get your free personality assessment and Investment Map at any time. Remember:

> *'He who knows others is learned.*
> *He who knows himself is wise.'*
> LAO TZU

If you're interested in learning more about enneagram assessments more generally, you can check out the resource listed in the reference notes.

## Personality goes a long way

When it comes to investing, the dominant line of thinking is that people are all sensible and coolly rational, and so no one ever loses control of their emotions. This could be singularly the most damaging belief when it comes to investing.

> *The reality is that when it comes to money,*
> *none of us are rational all the time.*

It simply doesn't add up that we can have a range of emotions — love, anger, sadness etc. — regarding a whole range of issues, but when it comes to money and investment, we all singularly take a rational approach. This is simply not true.

Many people, including some of those in the finance industry, believe that once they understand the 'facts' of the stock market they will be able to buy stocks when they fall and sell when they rise. It sounds so very simple! But putting this into action when there's money on the line is somewhat more difficult.

> *'What might seem irrational from the outside*
> *does not seem irrational from the inside.'*
> MARGARET H. SMITH

What stops us from doing this is our emotions. Any investment strategy that fails to account for an individual's beliefs and motivations will most likely fall short.

It's simply impossible to separate out our personality from our investing. Our personality combined with media headlines, investment advice and general fear and greed at specific points of the cycle all conspire to make investing difficult. When it comes to money, we tend to save, spend and invest for different reasons, and all of us have our own beliefs about money.

Some folks spend all their money on things they like (but may not necessarily need); others don't think much of saving and spend their money on family and friends before themselves. Others still impulse spend when they feel stressed or as a reward for achieving goals.

At the opposite end of the spectrum, some folks save as much as possible, even if they don't know what they are exactly saving for, and some are disciplined enough to save in order to achieve a financial goal. As such, we all possess strengths and weaknesses in our personalities that play a role when we invest.

But, as we are each somewhat different, we notice that when we explain our timeless investing concepts and principles there is a range of reactions.

*We all possess strengths and weaknesses in our personalities when we think about money and investments.*

*It's simply impossible to separate out our money and investment beliefs.*

Some people immediately understand the market cycles both at the 'head' level and at the intuitive level. Others hold strengths in different areas, such as diversification or risk management. Investment success relies heavily on knowing ourselves and how we prepare and react to changes in the stock market.

Using the 9 Types as a guide, we will be able to identify specific patterns of your personality and investing habits. The 9 Types can help to show your automatic patterns and unconscious biases most readily associated with your personality type. When combined with knowledge regarding the ebbs and flows of the stock market, understanding ourselves gives us a great advantage when it comes to successful investing.

Take the test in the appendix to find out what type of investor you are. Once you understand your type, you will be able to determine your strengths and weaknesses when it comes to investing. Then we can set about utilising those strengths and weaknesses to develop an Investment Map for you.

> *'The plan of betting only at the level that I was emotionally comfortable with — and not advancing until I was ready — enabled me to play my system with a calm and disciplined accuracy.'*
> ED THORP, LEGENDARY BILLIONAIRE
> INVESTOR AND AUTHOR

## Elements of decision-making

There are two major elements to your decision-making. One is your personality, and the second is the influence that your family, friends and the wider society play in your decision-making. In the stock market, it is important to recognise that your personality and the way you make decisions is an important ingredient in your success. We all tend to think we're unique and in many ways we are.

However, there are also many ways in which each of us is largely the same, and we often have more in common than we think.

> *As we are often fond of saying — we are the same but different.*

The 'same' part often includes that we generally all want a better life for ourselves, our children and our friends, and mostly we believe money has a key role to play in achieving that better life. The 'different' part is that because of our inherent beliefs about money as well as other things, what constitutes a better life is different for many of us. Because we each have a distinct personality, we each see money and the role it plays in our lives differently.

Some, like Steve, see money as the key to a life of freedom and, therefore, it is a way to deliver a life free from obligations and constraints, leaving us with a maximum of free time to spend how we want. Others may see money as a route to building wealth and significance and continue to work and achieve goals even though they have enough money to retire and do nothing. Still others will see money as something that you should share, and when they have money, they tend to be generous, especially to friends and others less fortunate than them.

Your specific personality combined with knowledge about the stock market or property market can play a role in your success (or failure). For example, while we necessarily don't enjoy market crashes, we do understand that these are excellent times to invest for the future and make solid investment returns. However, not everyone feels the same.

There are people who just won't invest because they think the stock market is inherently risky. Part of this is because they don't have the knowledge about how markets work, but it is also largely because of their individual personality and approach to risk.

> *As you can see, in the stock market, understanding your own personality and what you believe about money and markets can be critical to success.*

Stock markets are all about the risk/reward trade-off. Some of us are brave and carefree and happy to take risks if we believe the rewards are there. These folks tend to be classified as *risk-tolerant*. Others who are more cautious and focus on the risk side of the equation would be deemed more *risk-averse* or conservative. The truth is it's a continuum, rather than specific points.

For example, when you go to a financial advisor, they will ask you about your risk level as it's an important aspect of developing your investment strategy. However, most of us know little about our innate risk level and usually only understand more when we have some context.

We answer the question on risk along the lines of 'about the same as most people'. The problem here is twofold.

First, your risk level may be high or low because of your personality, but we aim to show you that should not play a large role in developing an investment strategy. The simple reason for this is that when the stock market is cheap, you should — if the cycles are understood properly — increase your investments rather than reduce them.

> *You should like low prices because there is a high likelihood that the future returns will be good.*

But investing when the market is declining is hard, not because of the numbers (cheaper stock prices usually leads to greater investment returns!), but because our personality and emotions unduly influence our investment approach.

Another challenge relates to timing. Our risk levels and feelings toward risk change with the prevailing circumstances. If you walked into a financial advisor's office and the stock market was all over the day's news due to a crash, you'd most likely say you were more risk-averse rather than risk-tolerant. Many financial advisors don't hear too often from their clients when the market is rising, but they're sure to hear from them when the market is falling!

*We all possess strengths and weaknesses
in our personalities when we think about
money and investments.*

*It is simply impossible to separate out
our money and investment beliefs.*

Investors who understand the market better would realise that in many cases it is their emotions that are dictating their approach towards investing. Therefore, we seek to understand our own personality and beliefs about risk and money. Once you understand your emotions, personality, motivations, strengths and weaknesses, you can recognise and understand your own behavioural patterns and those of others.

We can tell you that you won't achieve your optimum results when you don't think rationally about stocks. The idea of making decisions by 'gut feel' or intuition may pay off once or twice, but seldom does it work over an investment lifetime.

Firstly, it's not systematic and so there's a lack of consistency in your decision-making.

Secondly, gut feelings tend to ignore knowledge. Instead, you forego rational numbers and figures and accept stories about why certain investments might perform well in the future. In that case, you ignore stock market history and allow emotions, the media, and others influence to determine your decisions. If you make decisions this way, you are unlikely to succeed over time. As the old saying goes, the stock market is an expensive place to find out about yourself.

## Individual decision-making

As discussed above, personality heavily influences our approach to risk and stock markets and property markets. If you can understand what 'triggers' mistakes in your investing career, then you'll be a long way down the track to success. It's important to understand not only ourselves and how we make decisions (as the old sages say 'know thyself') but also how we came to make those decisions regarding how and what to invest in.

As social animals, we are each open to a considerable number of external influences in making decisions. Some are so subtle that we fail to realise just how influential the media and others are in our decision-making. In markets, people seldom come to investment decisions without being influenced by others.

## Decision-making and influences

Our personality and emotions such as fear and greed — combined with external influences such as the media and what we see, hear and read about what others are doing — all contribute to our investment decisions. Market bubbles and fads don't happen without an unhealthy dose of social contagion. Many decisions we make in daily life are unconscious, and we tend not to put much effort into them.

You generally don't spend large amounts of brainpower thinking about breakfast choices, for example. Most of us have some sort of morning routine that we repeat from Monday to Friday, and we may have a different routine for the weekend. If you think about it, advertising exists to influence — you could find that your chosen breakfast was due to advertising subtly driving you to choose certain products or alter your decisions and behaviour.

We only really put in effort when we need to make a decision that involves either stepping outside our normal routine, or when there are no generally agreed social norms about the issue at hand.

> *For example, the media play an enormous and influential role in the making of decisions.*

Every day there is stock market or property market reporting that is constantly influencing your thoughts and decisions about your investments. Most day-to-day reporting is 'noise', and it is not designed to inform you but simply get your attention. The problems can come when we start to feel the need to act on the information. Without principles and an overarching philosophy, you could potentially fall prey to any piece of information reported.

This can play havoc with decision-making because you are unwittingly letting your emotions be affected by what you read, hear and see. In the past decade or two, you'll have seen many folks follow a trend, whether it be tattoos, specific types of food (smashed avocado comes to mind!) or clothes (leggings and athleisure wear).

Humans tend to want to be part of the group, and so if the group starts to do something, then we tend to follow and adopt similar behaviour. Thus, we did not reach a decision to buy stocks all on our own. We most likely see a news article or friends start talking about a trend … it comes onto our radar, we see others doing it, and begin to think about whether we should too.

> **When it comes to investing, we are influenced by others.**

There's little worse than seeing a neighbour, relative or friend getting rich for what appears to be little effort. Therefore, we get fads and bubbles in property and stock markets.

We see others driving a new car after they told us how they much money they are making in the stock market, and so we decide to take ourselves off to the financial advisor. If 'that guy' next door can do it, so can I!

Here is a rough guide to how we make decisions:

**1.** We generally make decisions that require the least amount of effort. In our above example, this means not spending too much time deciding what to eat at breakfast every morning. You normally have cereal and coffee, and so there's no need to expend too much brainpower.

**2.** We also tend to adopt behaviour that is widely agreed to by most of society. In cases where there is a social norm, we tend to follow rather than again spending too much time searching for alternatives.

**3.** With regards to investing, we often check with family and friends first to see if they have any experience or whether they are invested in stocks or property. If they do, we follow along and, in many cases, start investing.

If our friends and family don't have the relevant experience, then we search wider until we have what we believe is the right amount of information about the subject. This might be a visit to a financial advisor or a decision to buy an investment book like this one. Many times, however, we have already decided (*'I'm buying a stock because my work colleague bought some and they're making money!'*), and we're simply going through the process of confirming that we have made the right decision.

Point three is where we often make mistakes because we don't look at the objective evidence. We tend to make the decision first and then confirm it, which is a process known as confirmation *bias*.

> *The problem for many is that they arrive late to the game, and so by the time they decide to buy, prices may be well above intrinsic value.*

They may end up buying close to the market top, not realising that it was those who bought cheaply that have made the profits. They take the plunge, not based on thorough research but the feeling that they know enough (*'it's safe!'*), and so they believe they too will do as well as their friends or family. Because markets cycle, a point too often forgotten, there will be many people who have bought at the wrong point in the cycle and so stand a greater probability of losing money.

This is because they haven't undertaken thorough research, understood market cycles, or developed a philosophy and set of rules and principles for investing. Predominantly they invested in something because it was in the media and their friends were doing it, and so they think that makes it safe.

The danger of social proof or contagion is that rational thinking and logic go out the window, and so social influence tends to push each of us in the same general direction. We think that this leads to safety, but in markets, it often leads to a less than critical appraisal of risk.

### 'Prices are rising, so what could go wrong?'

Rather than each as individuals making decisions based on both our personal circumstances and what we are truly comfortable with (our personality) we tend to follow the crowd. This is not to say following the crowd always leads to losses.

But because we understand there are good and bad times to invest due to market cycles (one of our other 8 timeless principles), you need to first be aware of where you are in the market cycle. And then you need to determine whether it is a good time to investigate further, rather than just mimicking the crowd.

Using market cycles along with our other principles leads to more effective decision-making with less influence from crowd groupthink or our own emotions.

# CHAPTER 9

# PRINCIPLE #3: MEAN REVERSION (& MACRO VALUATIONS)

## The law of averages

Imagine you are sitting in a cafe in your local area one weekend. And then imagine that over the time you drink your coffee, three people in a row walk in that are over seven feet tall. Would you, therefore, expect the next person who walks into the cafe to be over seven feet tall? Well, you *might*, due to recency bias!

Statistically, though, unless the Harlem Globetrotters are in town, it's unlikely to be the case! When it comes to averages and investing, you must try to think rationally rather than being swayed by recency bias, and trust in statistics over stories.

This is another relatively long chapter (the good news is it's the final long chapter in the book).

As before, if you struggle to absorb any of the information here, you can skip ahead to the next chapter. The key point to take away is that while markets can become very cheap or extremely expensive over time, they tend to revert towards an average level or 'mean'. To make money consistently you need to buy when markets are cheap. Much of the evidence that follows simply proves and reinforces this basic point.

## An introduction to mean reversion

Once you understand market cycles, then you need to be able to act upon them to deliver solid investment returns. There are two distinct parts to macro valuations. The first part involves thinking conceptually about market cycles and understanding the underlying forces that make markets cycle. This is where we think about mean reversion.

The second is how we use mean reversion to safeguard our capital, avoid potential losses, and make solid investment returns over the full market cycle.

*One of the most challenging parts of macro valuation is having some faith that markets will cycle (as they always have).*

It's psychologically difficult to see others making money in markets when the risk is high, while the earnings yield and expected future returns are declining. As humans, we mostly live in the here and now, and so we think a rising market is great. Even as an experienced full market cycle investor, you can come to feel that you are missing out on some of the 'easy' money.

But once you truly understand market cycles, you see that your asset allocation and rebalancing through the cycle are critical safeguards against substantial losses. Please keep that in mind when everyone around you is telling you how much they are making (or have made) without realising that they may be effectively picking up pennies in front of a steamroller. Remember, the route to wealth is through avoiding big losses!

Let's think about mean reversion.

Distribution of Australian stocks (ASX) returns by calendar year, grouped into return bands:

| < -23% | (-23% to -7%) | (-7% to 0%) | (0% to 7%) | (7% to 23%) | >23% |
|---|---|---|---|---|---|
|  |  |  |  | 2007 |  |
|  |  |  |  | 2006 |  |
|  |  |  |  | 2005 |  |
|  |  |  |  | 2004 |  |
|  |  |  |  | 2003 |  |
|  |  |  |  | 1999 |  |
|  |  |  |  | 1998 |  |
|  |  |  |  | 1997 |  |
|  |  |  |  | 1996 |  |
|  |  |  |  | 1995 |  |
|  |  |  |  | 1991 |  |
|  |  |  |  | 1989 |  |
|  |  |  |  | 1988 |  |
|  |  |  |  | 1978 |  |
|  |  |  |  | 1963 |  |
|  |  |  |  | 1958 |  |
|  |  |  | 2010 | 1957 |  |
|  |  |  | 2001 | 1954 |  |
|  |  |  | 2000 | 1953 |  |
|  |  |  | 1977 | 1947 |  |
|  |  |  | 1969 | 1946 |  |
|  |  |  | 1966 | 1945 |  |
|  |  |  | 1964 | 1942 |  |
|  |  |  | 1961 | 1936 |  |
|  | 2011 |  | 1956 | 1934 |  |
|  | 2002 |  | 1955 | 1933 |  |
|  | 1994 |  | 1949 | 1932 |  |
|  | 1990 |  | 1944 | 1931 |  |
|  | 1987 |  | 1943 | 1928 |  |
|  | 1982 |  | 1939 | 1926 | 2009 |
|  | 1981 |  | 1935 | 1925 | 1993 |
|  | 1971 |  | 1927 | 1924 | 1986 |
|  | 1970 |  | 1920 | 1923 | 1985 |
|  | 1965 |  | 1918 | 1922 | 1983 |
|  | 1960 | 1992 | 1914 | 1921 | 1980 |
|  | 1952 | 1984 | 1913 | 1919 | 1979 |
|  | 1951 | 1976 | 1912 | 1917 | 1975 |
|  | 1941 | 1962 | 1911 | 1909 | 1972 |
| 2008 | 1929 | 1948 | 1910 | 1908 | 1968 |
| 1974 | 1916 | 1940 | 1907 | 1905 | 1967 |
| 1973 | 1915 | 1938 | 1906 | 1903 | 1959 |
| 1930 | 1901 | 1937 | 1904 | 1902 | 1950 |

Source: Australian Securities Exchange

The graphic in figure 9.1 is a distribution of the annual returns of the Australian Securities Exchange (ASX). This looks very much like a normal distribution. There are some very good years, and there are some very bad years. Similarly, in the US the average or mean annual return of the S&P 500 is about 10%. However, it has only ever delivered 10% a handful of times in nearly 100 years of investing. There is considerable debate about using a normal distribution when discussing investment returns.

People seem to default to averages and standard deviations as tools when assessing returns. We think that there's enough evidence to show that you can use a normal distribution when looking at the longer term. What denotes the longer term is usually just a matter of common sense. We think the markets have been around long enough to see a majority of what can happen. There have been periods where international stock markets delivered triple-digit returns in a single year, and periods where losses have been well over 50% in a single year[1].

## Bull markets and bear markets

Everything tends to cluster in markets. Until it doesn't. Up days and down days cluster together. Weeks cluster. Months cluster. And years cluster. This leads to cyclical bull and bear markets. With regards to mean reversion, one must always think dynamically not statically.

*Mean reversion, or anti-persistence, is important to investing.*

Remember, those years of great returns are not very likely to continue forever. The problem is that most investors tend to think they will. Terrible stock market returns also don't continue forever. Although the number of up and down days stays relatively constant, the percentage changes are the important bit. Bear markets are followed by bull markets, and vice versa.

## The mean reversion principle

Mean reversion is possibly the most infuriating principle out of all of them, but if you ignore it, you will be punished. Although you can see it, and conceptually grasp it, it's still a source of frustration. As we know, it is somewhat difficult to predict the future. When you think about mean reversion, it usually happens when you least expect it, or when complacency has set in.

The market has risen for a few years, and so people just tend to think it will continue.

> *When someone discusses mean reversion,*
> *it often seems out of place.*

We think the reason why is because as humans, we prefer stories rather than numbers, and we also don't really grasp correlation all that well. It's because of mean reversion that we need to rebalance our investment portfolio to manage risk. Mean reversion is also partially responsible for why we need asset allocation decisions and diversification. Mean reversion does incorporate an element of chance or luck.

Golfers like Steve know mean reversion well. They set up at the tee and hit their drive. They miss the fairway but hit a tree and the ball rolls back on to the fairway.

Smile. They play on and get a par. Now, imagine the scenario if the same ball hits the tree and bounces into the water, or a parallel fairway?

No smile!

Par becomes a double bogey (note how many investors tell you about their skilful wins but not how lucky they are). Mean reversion and correlation are two sides of the same coin. Francis Galton discovered long ago that correlation and regression were not two different concepts but simply different perspectives on the same concept. The general rule is straightforward — whenever the correlation between two scores is imperfect (meaning a correlation figure of less than one), then there is mean reversion. This is very important for two reasons.

One, in markets, you need to understand that the price you pay is important (if it wasn't, then price would be irrelevant, and so you could buy any asset or stock at any price, and it would just continue upwards forever). And, two, it also means that the best time to buy is when the price of an asset is below the mean.

And the further away from the mean, the better.

## Choose statistics over stories

The hard part about mean regression or reversion is that it is counterintuitive. Most folks get caught in a trend that they reason will go on forever. But feeling both positive and negative can be deadly. We tend to let recency bias dominate our immediate outlook and thoughts and use emotionally based references for our investment decisions. Think how often we see property investors piling into markets at the peak of a boom!

Why does this happen? As John Maynard Keynes said:

*'The existing situation enters, in a sense disproportionately, into the formation of our long-term expectations; our usual practice being to take the existing situation and to project it into the future.'*

People remember the recent past better than the distant past, and so they generally act on the latest information without considering the full history (a bias called *representativeness*). They assume that companies that have done well over the past two or three years will continue to do so, and companies that have disappointed over the same timeframe will continue to disappoint.

Representativeness is where the investor sees the results as 'typical' and ignores reversion to the mean and the laws of probability. When a company has a consistent history of earnings growth over several years, accompanied as it may be by salient and enthusiastic descriptions of its products and management, investors might conclude that the history is representative of the underlying earnings growth potential.

We humans prefer stories rather than statistics. Stories give meaning: they connect what appear to be separate events. They flow logically from the previous information, and so we tend to grasp stories more easily than numbers.

Numbers are dry. No one argues that one plus one equals anything other than two. But stories can be discussed and disputed and feed our need for interaction with other people (it's worth noting that algorithms are better than humans because they don't have feelings and they don't succumb to 'stories'— they just look at the hard data). We argue that you will generate better investment returns if you give numbers a higher weighting than stories.

## Correlation is not causation

Correlation is not causation! This is a really important point with regards to mean regression.

Because we prefer stories over statistics and as humans, we seek a cause (or a meaning) for all events ... but we fail to understand mean reversion. The below example from Daniel Kahneman's *Thinking Fast and Slow* encapsulates the idea succinctly.

Depressed children treated with an energy drink will often see their condition improve. This may be true, but it doesn't necessarily mean that the drink caused the improvement. Mean reversion holds that some of the children would have improved regardless. Which is why you need a control group to determine if the drink improved them more than regression alone.

Luck can also close the gap between good and bad performance because luck is most likely the cause of the gap in the first place. The average gap must shrink, and this is the regression to the mean[2].

*Recognising numbers over stories is a key behavioural trait of successful investors.*

## Temporary versus permanent states

Many investors mistake a trend for a direction and a new 'permanent' state (of wealth). But a trend is simply a by-product of the fluctuations, variation or volatility within a domain or system like the S&P 500 index. Variation in one part of the system is often mistaken for an overall trend.

Say 'the market' is believed to be trending upwards, but it is only tech stocks (and a small portion of them) that are providing the gains. The variation among the sectors will unduly influence the whole. For example, tech, finance and telecoms may boom, which distorts the returns to the whole market.

Their outperformance pushes the whole market higher. This is often interpreted as a strong overall move, when in fact it is not. But this is only understood by looking at the variation, not the average. Most stocks can decline, yet their decline can be offset by an outsized performance in a small minority of stocks. This is the issue with the rise of the market — investors believe that there is 'progress' and so believe they are richer than they are.

However, if you view the market as a cycle rather than a 'thing heading somewhere' (implying direction and a new permanent state), then you can interpret the change (either up or down) as neither positive nor negative. It simply depends on what position in the cycle you're in.

If you view it as a cycle, then you are neither positive nor negative about the current 'direction'. The mistake we make is to see the market as a 'thing' that is moving somewhere (what Gould calls progress — refer to the next section), when, in fact, it is simply change or variation (of individual companies that comprise the system) within a system. If the whole economy is strong, then most stocks will do well.

But if there is one sector outperforming, then the market may well be higher, when in fact conditions are worse for most companies. If the system's underlying structure is the same, then the system has not changed — only in the way investors think at that moment. It has simply undergone some variation that investors mistake for a trend. And the results will be the same and follow previous patterns — hence, we get mean reversion. Certain sectors (or countries when talking about the global economy) temporarily outperform, which drags up the whole market.

## Gould's 'Spread of Excellence'

If the system stays the same, meaning there's no structural change, then the results will be the same. If there are no changes to the way the stock market operates, then the return pattern or flows of the market will fluctuate around the long-term mean (8–10%) rather than go anywhere 'new' on a permanent basis. To reiterate, most investors seem to think that the market going up is 'progress' (and a new higher never-ending plateau) or defining direction, when the reality is that it should be viewed as simply a temporary fluctuation within the overall system.

*A cycle.* It is simply volatility (change), which is represented by numbers. The challenge comes in determining the timeframe. The only way to have no mean reversion would be to have a permanent state of change whereby the economy never experienced any downturns ... even minor ones. In that case, we would have to end the business cycle.

Price would not be an issue because no matter what you paid, there would be no chance (risk) of a loss. And people would be devoid of emotion. We should be studying variation in the entire system and its changing pattern of spread through time. Trends should not be viewed as something moving somewhere but properly viewed as results of expanding or contracting variation, rather than concrete entities moving in a definite direction.

Variation is the true reality.

### *Average is an abstraction.*

If the stock market was to undergo a permanent change, then the mean would be higher (or lower) on a permanent basis — this means there would have to be a new 'law of large numbers' distribution in order to alter the previous one. The stock market is also an indicator for the economy, and you can't have the market getting ahead of the economy on any type of permanent basis.

*Therefore, mean reversion is a certainty;*
*it is simply a matter of timing.*

Thus we need to look at a few things:

If the returns are made up of changes in the P/E (via inflation) or earnings (via economic growth) or dividends, then there would need to be permanent changes in one or more of these factors. This is slightly different for an individual company — they may grow or scale, though even an individual company must slow down eventually, as they cannot experience exponential growth forever.

*Trees don't grow to the sky.*

If mean reversion is a given, and the key to profiting from it is timing, then you must next look at the risk hierarchy and determine what the level of risk is in each investment. As we have said, an individual company is riskier than a sector, which is somewhat riskier than a country, which is riskier than the world. Individual companies might blow up, but countries and sectors can represent more diversified investments for you.

'This time it's different' is a popular saying in the stock market. However, the truth is that there is seldom a change of such proportion that places us on a new path or that 'we are standing at the precipice of a new dawn'. You will hear about the changes that the motor car, the aeroplane and the Internet made on society — revolutions! — but still, they didn't stop the stock market cycles.

## Progress is just change

Because bull markets go on for longer than we expect, we tend to question whether something has changed, and then we set about looking for that 'something' (confirmation bias). The challenge is determining the timeframe, and this is where initial *asset allocation* comes in, as it assists you to reduce risk in case you are wrong. It does this by feeding in money and lowering your overall purchase price. If mean reversion exists, then it is simply a matter of not running out of money. There are different ways to allocate your money, which we'll look at, including the *Kelly criterion*.

## Mean reversion in action

Over the very long term, the average return from the stock market has been somewhere between 8-12%. If over five years the stock market returns 20%, 18%, 19%, 15% and 17%, then it is likely that over the next few years the returns will be lower in order to counterbalance the recent greater than average returns.

In some years the return will be lower and some years the returns will be higher, but over the long term they have averaged out to about 12%. Take the energy sector — if you had bought it at the lows, at the end of 2016, you would be very happy. Now imagine telling your friends that oil and energy is the place to be at the lows. Yes, a place where past two-year losses had been approximately 50%, and disaster headlines and predictions of alternative energy takeover were everywhere.

The same thing happens with countries falling in and out of favour. Buying when everyone is despondent about an individual stock, sector, country or style is tough. But it can be hugely rewarding. How do you use this knowledge in your investment approach?

Consider this: if mean reversion is 'real' and exists in markets, which it has been proven to do, then you want to be buying when valuations are on the 'low' side, not the 'high' side! If the average annual return going forward is approximately 8–10%, then you want to be buying when the recent returns have been lower or negative.

Why? Because mean reversion works, then you will generate outsized returns as the market reverts.

## Trees don't grow to the sky

There is considerable evidence to show that markets undergo mean reversion. Mean reversion can be applied to a large range of economic data (trees don't grow to the sky) and to each of the asset classes. We aim to show you how you can use mean reversion most effectively in your investing in the stock market. Below is some academic support regarding why you need to account for mean reversion when thinking about the stock market.

## Profit and general economic data

There is a wealth of data, as studied by value investor James Montier, to show that profits are mean-reverting as well as markets. In a 2000 study, French and Fama found that profitability was mean-reverting at the rate of approximately 40% per year. In addition to this, Montier also noted that the rate of mean reversion is higher when profitability is far from its mean (in either direction), or the rate of reversion is higher when profitability is below the mean.

Prices of 'glamour' stocks are therefore likely to reflect the failure of investors to impose mean reversion on growth forecasts. In layman's terms, this means that a company makes a good profit announcement, so people buy their shares expecting greater profits in the future. This also happens partly because analysts and the company announce a brighter future. The share price rises and so more people buy shares. The company continues in the short term to make profits, and this apparently confirms to people that their investment is a sound one.

But historically after making a great profit, and as a result of human nature, companies start to make less successful investment decisions or become complacent, and so after a period (usually about three years), profits start to decline back to the mean$_3$. Thus, the prior success is followed by mean reversion as a result of internal company actions. External changes such as increased competition or changes in the broader market also contribute to mean reversion.

More broadly there is substantial evidence for Templeton's belief that you should buy at the time of maximum pessimism and sell at the time of maximum optimism. So as Horace said:

> *'Many shall be restored that are now fallen;*
> *and many shall fall that now are in honour.'*

There's no doubt some individual companies can defy the law of mean reversion for long periods. While a consistent pattern of high growth may be nothing more than a random draw for a lucky few firms, investors see 'order among the chaos' and infer that the company will just simply keep on growing. Thus, people's representativeness bias might disregard the reality that a history of high earnings growth has a low probability of repeating itself. They will overvalue the company and be disappointed in the future as the earnings growth fails to materialise.

## Mean reversion in individual stocks

Other studies have confirmed the existence of mean reversion. In their article *'A Model of Investor Sentiment'*, Barberis, Shleifer and Vishny state that over a one-to 12-month period, share prices typically underreact to news. And consequently, news is only slowly incorporated into share prices that tend to exhibit positive auto-correlations over these time periods. Thus, current good news has power in predicting positive returns in the short term.

But over time periods of three to five years, share prices tend to overreact to consistent patterns of news pointing in the same direction. That is, stocks that experience a long period of good news tend to become overpriced (from all the recent good news), and then have low average returns afterwards.

> *After a period, they revert*
> *to the mean.*

Unfortunately, for many people, they read a good report on the company from the media or the company itself, and assuming the good times will continue, buy the shares. This is a case of representativeness — using only the most recent information as part of their decision-making. We see similar same patterns that we see in nature and in culture — reversion to the mean[4]. Studies show over a two or three-year period, yesterday's laggards become tomorrow's leaders and vice versa[5].

To exploit this flaw of intuitive forecasts, contrarian or value investors should sell stocks that have experienced high growth in the recent past and buy stocks that have experienced low growth in the recent past. When shares are selected on price changes over the prior three years, we see that the high-flyers (the loved stocks that everyone is buying) fall back to earth, and the 'losers' (the stocks that everyone sold) rise. There are many studies to show that this is the case.

In their article 'Does the Stock Market Overreact?', Werner, De Bondt and Thaler show that over the past 50 years 'loser' stocks outperformed the market by an average 19.6% three years after their purchase. 'Winners' on the other hand, earned about 5% less than the average market return. A more recent study by Statman et al. covered a period from 1986 to 2006. They found that the 'loser' stocks outperformed the 'winner' stocks in terms of their long-term investment value by approximately 2% per year. This is important: the big returns (or gains that see the stock price revert to its intrinsic value) often happen within 12 to 24 months from the formation of the portfolio.

As could be expected if you buy stocks when the market is low, it may take some time before they rise again.

## Developed markets and mean reversion

A study used indexes from 1971 and ETFs from 1997 to show that mean reversion exists in country indexes. The study covered 45 developed and emerging markets. The strategy was loosely based on the Dogs of the Dow strategy of buying the out of favour or highest yielding stocks, but also the MOAR (Michael O'Higgins Absolute Return). It essentially allocates 4% to each of the cheapest five stock markets.

The benchmark is the global index. If an index in the portfolio declines after one year then another 4% is added to them. In other words, the investor adds more to the investments if they decline. This means you need to hold some cash to be able to implement such a strategy.

The strategy invests over a five-year holding period.
The first part is where 20% of the funds are invested in the bottom five markets. The next year another 20% is invested in the bottom five, the next year another 20%, and so on until year five. At the start of year six, the first-year investments are cashed in.

*This means the strategy is a rolling one ... for all markets.*

Here's what the study found. A one-year holding period was found to be too short to be effective. Three-year to five-year holding periods were found to be more effective for performance. If you were to follow such a strategy, there's no need to invest in the five cheapest markets. The cheapest two, three or four markets could also work. Using the ETF strategy that we propose is cheap and easy to implement.

We also believe there is generally less risk in investing in ETFs than there is in selecting individual companies and forming a port-folio. One of the findings of such studies is that there can be a higher level of volatility due to the investment selected (but remember, volatility is not the same thing as risk!). The mean reversion principle applies to individual stocks, asset classes, industry sectors and national markets. The level of mean reversion often reflects how large the prior extreme event was. A bit like third law of motion, a large decline in the market is typically followed by an equally large and opposite reaction.

## Emerging markets and mean reversion

Another study was undertaken to determine if mean reversion happens in emerging markets from 1985 to 2002. And the results, which we've replicated out until 2019, showed that mean reversion of country indexes also takes place in emerging markets. Thus, this is a strategy that works in developed markets and emerging markets. Next, let's look at …

## Industry sectors from 1926 to 1998

Our findings here were that portfolio prices revert to their fundamental levels after a temporary shock.

*That is, once again, stock prices are mean-reverting.*

Using what is known as a parametric contrarian investment strategy (in plainer English, essentially portfolio switching) results in outperformance, which confirms an earlier study done by Thaler and De Bondt. It's important to note that the shock event must be temporary rather than permanent. This means that entire industry sectors and country indexes are likely to be more reliable investments than individual stocks, as they involve more than just one company. It is rare that a whole sector would be in permanent decline from a one-time event. However, individual companies can suffer a permanent decline. That is why Buffett buys large companies with a long and profitable history — because the chances of a permanent decline are much lower.

The same could be said for the Dogs of the Dow strategy (picking the recent worst-performing stocks) — you need to determine if the company in question can withstand the 'temporary' event. A company with low or no debt and solid fundamentals often entails less risk.

## Back to the golf course!

As you might have gathered, Steve likes his golf. So here's another golfing analogy from him (a short one, we promise!).

A simple example: Tiger Woods and I set up at the par-3 tee and hit our drive. Mine hits a rock to the side of the green and rolls on to the green a foot from the hole. Tiger hits the same rock, but his ball bounces in the opposite direction and into the lake.

I win the hole. You would not be thinking Steve is a better golfer than Tiger. I was just lucky on one hole. Over the course of the whole game, Tiger would most likely win by a large margin. Why? Because it was luck, not skill, that won me the par-3 hole.

## Mean reversion takes time

The tricky part of mean reversion is the timing of it. No one can say with great precision when the market will turn, but there's some comfort in knowing that it will. If your question is *'Well, that's great Pete and Steve, but how do I take advantage?'* then the answer lies in asset allocation and rebalancing your portfolio (and we'll show you why in our four action principles). In markets, this means that when you say there's mean reversion, it can be important to understand that it may take some time. Thus, if you forecast a mean reversion in an asset class, you stand a good chance of being wrong for what could possibly be a while.

There's no inherent time limit for mean reversion to take place. The hard part about mean reversion or regression is that it's counterintuitive. Most folks get caught in a trend that they reason will go on forever. But feeling both too positive and negative can stunt returns.

> *Remember, we humans prefer stories*
> *rather than statistics.*

Stories give meaning: they connect what appear to be separate events. They just seem to make sense to us. Every day, commentators sell stories and give in-depth explanation regarding the day's events. Stock market reporting is no different. The more the market moves, the more excitable or panicky the explanations get. But there's rarely any proof that these stories are correct in explaining the stock market's movements. Because we tend to prefer stories to numbers, most of us settle for these explanations rather than seek out other potential reasons ourselves. Compared to stories, which people tend to like, the numbers just come across as dry.

In some ways, they don't seem to tell you much.

*Yep, one plus one equals two. Yawn.*

But put a bunch of words together, and you get a story that can have all sorts of meaning and emotions attached to it. Companies use qualitative and quantitative details numbers in their regular reports to shareholders. Accordingly, most company annual reports start out with a chairman's statement regarding the past performance and some discussion of the way forward. The numbers come after the chairman has set the scene. But you should give preference, or at least an equal weighting, to the statistics.

Remember, algorithms are better than humans because they don't have feelings! There are no stories, and so they outperform in many cases by simply looking at the numbers. When the numbers 'appear' horrible, usually a result of some stories regarding prospects, the algorithm ignores all that and simply buys if the numbers fit the algorithm's criteria. Developing a systematic process for buying and selling stocks is the equivalent of having an algorithm do the work.

Many successful investors use algorithm type processes (and we will too) that ignore stories surrounding potential investments.

They are wise enough to know that stories are subjective and prone to be repeated by people who have not done their homework or by those who fail to account for the potential mean reversion.

## Trends, mean reversion and base rates

As stated, mean reversion is a statistical phenomenon. Think about this. The average annual return (the mean) over around 90 years for the Australian stock market (ASX) is roughly 10%. (the geometric mean is actually 6%).

However, the market seldom returns exactly 10%. The chart below shows that 10% falls within the 7% to 23% return range, and while there are a good number of returns within that range, there are very few that are exactly 10%.

## FIGURE 9.2 – DISTRIBUTION OF RETURNS

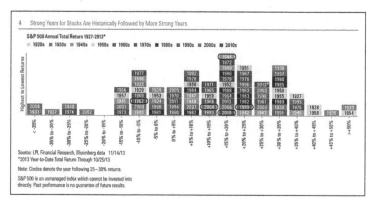

Source: Bloomberg

We can see that although the overall market may average a return of around 10%, the annual returns vary considerably from year to year. And within an annual return, there will be variations between the different sectors.

And finally, within the sector, there are individual companies that show different returns. Now you might well ask which the companies or sectors are, or even years, to choose in order to maximise the probability of success, because where you start is critical in terms of measuring the degree of success in your investments.

*Essentially you want to buy cheap,*
*avoid the losers, and sell expensive.*

Given that we know that over a long period of time that the overall average returns will be approximately 8–10%, then we start to get a feeling that we should be looking at the cheaper end of the market for potential sources of mean reversion and outperformance.

Next, we can look at which sectors may have underperformed not only their own long term average return, but also have been beaten by the other sectors in the market (this has to occur as it is rare that all sectors will rise or fall by exactly the same percentage of a year). It's natural that some sectors are more in favour than others.

Then we could look at that sector's companies to select a potential mean reversion candidate, or simply buy an ETF that covers the whole sector. This is a strategy favoured by David Dreman, a successful US fund manager. Dreman shows that you can get great outperformance if you select the best company — by his criteria — in the recently **worst performing** industry[6].

## Mean reversion timeframes

To recap, one trick used by investment advisors and fund managers is to quote their annual average returns. Average returns may be useful, but they don't always apply.

Where you start in the market cycle and the market's valuation are critical to investment success. That's because if the stock market has recently experienced three to five years of great returns above 10% (or well above 10%), then you should be cautious and expect that at some stage the future returns will revert to the long-term mean.

For example, if the overall returns for the past five years were 100%, then the recent average is 20%. But you know the long-term average is closer to 10%, so you would expect some mean reversion in the future. While the market may continue to return 10% for a while, that doesn't mean regardless of when you start and finish your return will average 10% per year. So be alert when investment advisors and fund managers quote average annual returns.

*Buying when everyone is despondent about an individual stock, sector, country or style is tough.*

But it is rewarding!

## CAPE ratio

The market timing mechanism we prefer to use is simple, effective and has a strong track record of protecting your capital (our first job) and delivering solid investment returns (our second job). It is called the CAPE ratio and it stands for the Cyclically Adjusted Price Earnings ratio. It was developed by Robert Shiller, although Ben Graham, the godfather of value investing, discussed a very similar concept many decades earlier in his book *Security Analysis*[7]

There are many macro valuation indicators, but we've found that generally when the CAPE is indicating cheap (or expensive) markets, then most other macro valuation indicators are indicating something similar. There may be differences, but generally, it's a matter of degree rather than outrightly contradicting the CAPE.

The main criticism (which usually comes from the finance industry because they like buy-and-hold) is that the CAPE ratio could cause you to miss out on some of the upside from market cycles, by causing you to sell too early. Finance folks seem to forget past market declines — if you think you are missing out then you are probably not looking at the full market cycle.

> *Investing should be treated as a business —*
> *its constant objective to produce profits*
> *while remaining respectful of adverse*
> *periods and conditions.*

The argument about CAPE is really an argument between those who say you can't time the market and those who say, yes, you can time the market. Out of all the disagreements in investing, this one is probably the most contentious.

Briefly:

**Time in the market** — advocates say that it's impossible to time the market by selling at the top and buying at the bottom.

The best returns are delivered by simply holding stocks for a long time, and you should be rewarded with the long-term average of around 8% to 10% (figures we know are not strictly accurate).

**Timing the market** — advocates say that there are stock market indicators and ratios that reveal times when markets are cheap, and you should allocate accordingly, or expensive, when you should minimise your allocation to stocks. Our assumption is that you won't pick the exact top or bottom, but you can get close enough so that market timing delivers better returns than buy-and-hold.

Who's right? If you look at stock market history, you will find that the greatest damage to your portfolio is when the market suffers large losses. It does this on a regular basis, and sometimes, like in the early 1990s recession or 2007–08, the losses can be extremely damaging.

Look at the Australian ASX 300 (Australia's top 300 listed companies). In 2007, the ASX peaked at approximately 6,500. It then crashed in the GFC to a low of approximately 3,500. As of the end of 2019, the ASX had just about returned to the 2007 peak.

That's a lot of lost ground to make up over a dozen years, and for the most case, investor returns before dividends are a little better because they continue to place funds in the markets at the lower prices via their superannuation and using the concept of dollar-cost averaging.

Quite rightly those who believe in buy-and-hold, which is most of the finance industry, will say we're choosing specific dates. And that's true. If you select March 2009 to February 2019, thus missing the big losses, you will have nearly doubled your money before dividends.

### But that would be timing the market!

If you're in a bear market, then you may not make any profits from your passive approach. Benign neglect can be positive when you are in a long-term (secular) bull market, but not in a long-term bear market. It is unwise to be 100% invested in the market at every point in time.

We favour timing the market using CAPE because there is sufficient historical data that reveals that while you will not sell at the exact market peak or buy at the market low (no one actually does this is reality anyway), there are indicators that can reveal when the market is getting expensive and when it's cheap. The Shiller CAPE ratio is one among a few that has a very good track record of showing when risk is high and when it is low.

**FIGURE 9.3 – CAPE RATIOS**

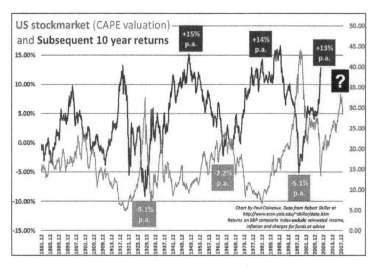

Source: Paul Claireaux

In bull markets like the 1982 to 2000 bull market, the returns from buy-and-hold were tremendous at approximately 16% per annum.

But the crucial point is that the stock market was signalling how 'cheap' it was from the late 1970s. When it crashed in 2000, the same indicator reveals that the market was crazily expensive. From

2000 to 2019, the buy-and-hold returns have been underwhelming, to say the least. Buying when the whole market is cheap pays off handsomely. Now look at the losses (also known as drawdowns) in the following chart.

Note how the average losses are larger when the Shiller CAPE ratio is high and well above the long-term average of approximately 16.

**FIGURE 9.4 – AVERAGE AND MAXIMUM DRAWDOWNS**

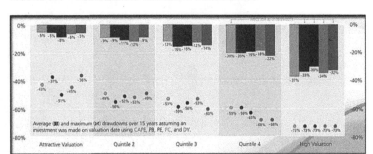

The point is often made by those that don't favour timing (most financial advisors don't like timing because that means less money and income for them) that you can't pick the top. But it's not necessary to pick the top exactly. You simply need to adjust your exposure as the market rises and so at the market 'top', you have little invested and more in cash for when the market inevitably declines.

John Templeton was famous — and still is among investors — for his great wisdom and stock market returns. When Templeton speaks on stock market investing, we should all take note. Here's how he allocated his client's money to the market. Note that as the market rose, Templeton accumulated more and more cash waiting for the inevitable decline.

**FIGURE 9.5 – ALLOCATION TO STOCKS**

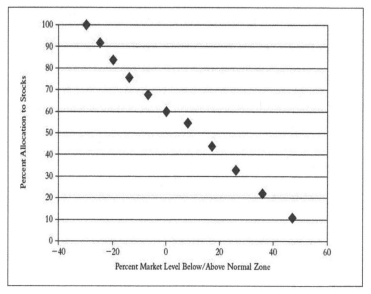

Source: Meb Faber

When the stock market was trading more than 60% above its 'normal' level, the proportion in stocks should be reduced to zero. When stocks were trading more than 30% below normal, the allocation to stocks for the average client could theoretically rise to as much as 100%. Templeton is simply pointing out that buy-and-hold is dangerous because the market eventually reverts to its long-term average.

But we know the long-term average is made up of bull markets and bear markets, and so your returns can vary depending on when you buy and when you sell. As with many things in life, if the risk of a loss, damage or injury is high then it warrants more caution and in the case of the stock market, this means holding more cash. Many investors don't like holding cash, especially when the market continues to march northward, but the reality is that all bull markets are followed by bear markets and vice versa.

It is important to understand this fact because holding cash eventually can be deployed to earn higher returns.

Patience!

*You have $10,000 and a choice — invest today and earn 7% a year for 10 years or leave your money in cash earning 4% (a normal rate under most conditions) for four years, and then invest in a stock earning 10% for the next six years.*

*Waiting patiently for that 10% opportunity yields dramatic results.*

*After 10 years, you would have 16% more money.*

*If you simply sat on your cash for four years waiting for a great opportunity.*

Too many folks get carried away with the gains, get lazy with their portfolio since it has increased a lot and then believe that it will always rise or not fall a lot like in 2007–08. Before you get lost in the time/timing argument, ask yourself is the broader market in a secular bull or secular bear market? Indicators like the Shiller CAPE ratio can help you manage your portfolio to avoid heavy losses while at the same time enjoying most of the profits. Here's an example of why you need cash available when the market declines to attractive levels.

## Summary of mean reversion

Mean reversion is real, and it exists in markets. In order to profit from it, you need to buy low and sell high. If the average annual return is approximately 8–10%, then you want to be buying when the returns have been lower or even negative.

Why? Because mean reversion works, and then you will generate outsized returns as the market reverts. It takes some fortitude to be able to do that, and you may suffer some 'pain' after you initially buy. But in combination with a sensible asset allocation plan and a rebalancing plan, you will increase the probability of enjoying solid investment returns.

# CHAPTER 10

# PRINCIPLE #4: THE RISK HIERARCHY

## The most important thing about risk?

Much about being a successful investor in all markets comes down to risk. Intuitively, you already know a lot about risk and impact. For example, you know that you could probably dodge your way through traffic and get across a busy road without waiting for the green man to signal that it's now safe to cross.

You *could* ... but the benefits are relatively low, and there's also a risk of you being killed! Therefore, you don't do it! Not if you're sensible, at any rate. Traditionally business schools have taught students to consider a risk matrix, as follows:

**FIGURE 10.1 – RISK MATRIX**

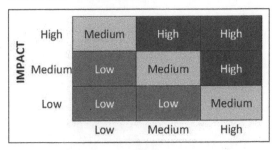

Successful and sustainable investing through market cycles and all conditions is about generating acceptable returns without taking on high risks. Unfortunately, we see people taking on a high risk of loss all the time. In property we see amateur property developers taking on millions of dollars of debt for an assumed 10% or 20% return. This type of approach can be risky: it works until it doesn't, and then you get killed.

Academic papers have tended to define risk as volatility, but we see things differently.

**Volatility is <u>not</u> the same thing as risk.**

Remember, we've never seen anyone complain about volatility when markets are rising!

**Risk really pertains to a permanent loss of capital.**

Now if you invest in individual companies, there's always some risk of a permanent loss of capital. The average lifespan of a listed company these days is surprisingly short. Quite often businesses become insolvent, or they are merged, or they're taken over.

For a business that becomes insolvent or goes bust, the stock price may hit zero, and there's no coming back from that point. The capital you invest in such a company is permanently lost.

There will be no mean reversion. This is where the risk hierarchy principle comes in.

There have been great developments in investment products over recent years, so that if you don't want to invest in individual companies you don't have to. And, in fact, as we will show, if you buy whole indexes when they are cheap, you can generate strong enough returns without needing to invest in individual companies. In other words, you can get to the desired destination without the risk of being killed!

## The risk hierarchy principle

Every investor should ultimately seek the holy grail: an investment strategy that entails low risk but delivers high returns. Unfortunately, too many forget about the risk side of the equation! After 20 years as investors, we believe that successful investing is more about avoiding losses than it is in trying to find the next big winner.

### *Risk is about loss of capital.*

Warren Buffett's first rule of investment is 'don't lose money', and his second rule is 'remember rule number one'. Investing is all about outlaying money today with a plan to get more back in the future, however short or distant that future may be. When we speak of risk, we are really talking about possible future outcomes. Risk, in order to be a useful concept in investing — or in most situations — must firstly have a context to it.

In other words, it's a subjective proposition rather than an objective (numbers-based) one. Most investments are not a 50/50 proposition. Remember it's all about finding asymmetrical bets, meaning that there's a difference between the pay-off probabilities and the risk. That requires us to look and wait patiently for situations or investment opportunities that are asymmetrical. Let's look again at the lifetime returns from individual stocks.

## FIGURE 10.2 – LIFETIME RETURNS FROM INDIVIDUAL STOCKS

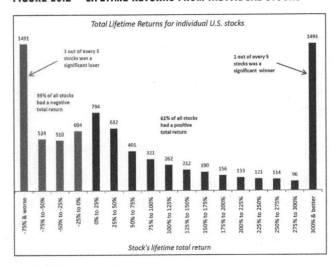

And let's remember what we first considered in chapter 4:

- Two out of every five stocks are a losing money investment (39%).
- Nearly one out of every five of stocks lost at least 75% of their value (18.5%).
- 64% of stocks underperformed the Russell 3000 during their lifetime.
- A small minority significantly outperformed their peers.
- Fat tails — one out of five was significant winner and loser.

Index returns *may* (or may not) be lower, but so is the risk! Therefore, we must use what we call the risk hierarchy. With an adequate time horizon, the least risk is probably achieved buying 'the whole market'. All stock markets crash, but most, if not all, recover in time.

If we can produce a risk hierarchy for investing, it would look something like this — going from low risk to high risk:

**1.** Purchasing all countries (a global) indexes ETF.
**2.** Purchase a single country index using ETFs.
**3.** A single sector/industry/style using ETFs.
**4.** A portfolio consisting of individual stocks.
**5.** A single company's stock.

This is not set in stone as there are many permutations, but it at least provides some framework for assessing potential risk and returns. Therefore, Buffett says that if you don't know what you're doing, buy an index, due to the reduced risk. Rather interestingly, the returns that you can generate from purchasing a single country's index or a single sector can be quite substantial.

And the risk is much reduced from buying a portfolio of individual stocks. Now have a look again at the quilt of returns from international stock markets. Pay attention to the returns for each of the countries in their best years. They are very impressive!

And most are delivered when in the immediately preceding years they were hated (remember: buy low, sell high).

## FIGURE 10.3 – INTERNATIONAL STOCK MARKET RETURNS

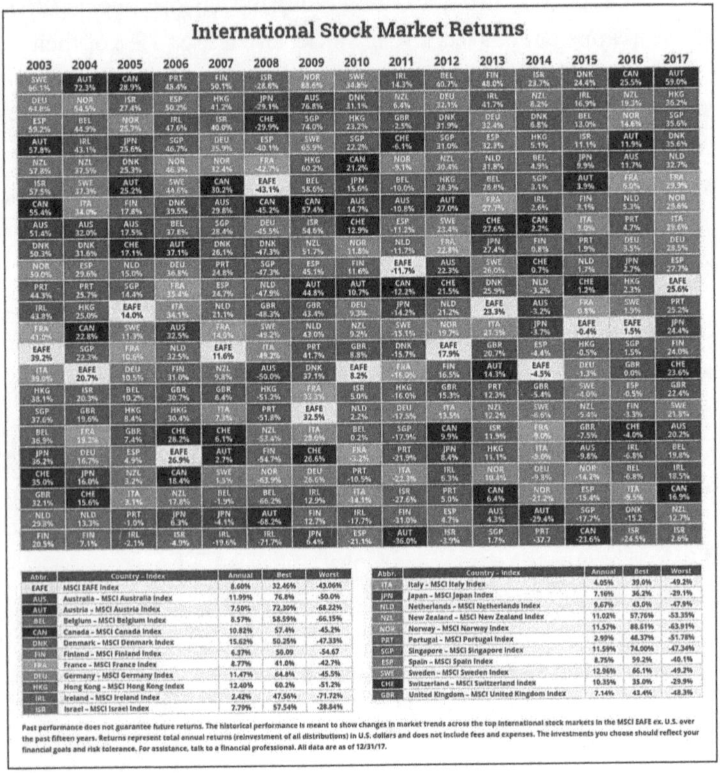
International Stock Market Returns
2003 2004 2005 2006 2007 2008 2009 2010 2011 2012 2013 2014 2015 2016 2017
Abbr. | Country – Index | Annual | Best | Worst
EAFE | MSCI EAFE Index | 8.60% | 32.46% | -43.06%
AUS | Australia – MSCI Australia Index | 11.99% | 76.8% | -50.0%
AUT | Austria – MSCI Austria Index | 7.50% | 72.30% | -68.22%
BEL | Belgium – MSCI Belgium Index | 8.57% | 58.59% | -66.15%
CAN | Canada – MSCI Canada Index | 10.82% | 57.4% | -45.2%
DNK | Denmark – MSCI Denmark Index | 15.62% | 50.25% | -47.33%
FIN | Finland – MSCI Finland Index | 6.37% | 50.09 | -54.67
FRA | France – MSCI France Index | 8.77% | 41.0% | -42.7%
DEU | Germany – MSCI Germany Index | 11.47% | 64.8% | -45.5%
HKG | Hong Kong – MSCI Hong Kong Index | 12.40% | 60.2% | -51.2%
IRL | Ireland – MSCI Ireland Index | 2.42% | 47.56% | -71.72%
ISR | Israel – MSCI Israel Index | 7.79% | 57.54% | -28.84%
ITA | Italy – MSCI Italy Index | 4.05% | 39.0% | -49.2%
JPN | Japan – MSCI Japan Index | 7.16% | 36.2% | -29.1%
NLD | Netherlands – MSCI Netherlands Index | 9.67% | 43.0% | -47.9%
NZL | New Zealand – MSCI New Zealand Index | 11.02% | 57.76% | -53.35%
NOR | Norway – MSCI Norway Index | 11.57% | 88.61% | -63.91%
PRT | Portugal – MSCI Portugal Index | 2.99% | 48.37% | -51.78%
SGP | Singapore – MSCI Singapore Index | 11.59% | 74.00% | -47.34%
ESP | Spain – MSCI Spain Index | 8.75% | 59.2% | -40.1%
SWE | Sweden – MSCI Sweden Index | 12.96% | 66.1% | -49.2%
CHE | Switzerland – MSCI Switzerland Index | 10.35% | 35.0% | -29.9%
GBR | United Kingdom – MSCI United Kingdom Index | 7.14% | 43.4% | -48.3%
Past performance does not guarantee future returns. The historical performance is meant to show changes in market trends across the top international stock markets in the MSCI EAFE ex. U.S. over the past fifteen years. Returns represent total annual returns (reinvestment of all distributions) in U.S. dollars and does not include fees and expenses. The investments you choose should reflect your financial goals and risk tolerance. For assistance, talk to a financial professional. All data are as of 12/31/17.

Source: Novel Investor

There are only a few simple questions you need to consider rather than sifting through endless financial statements.

Will a country go bankrupt? It's rare.

You can apply a similar methodology to sectors — because sectors too fall in and out of favour. Our point is again to remind you how important reversion to the mean is in investing. It's another reminder that buying assets when they look disastrous (buy low, sell high) and have performed badly, usually go on to outperform the recent best performers.

Of course, you can try to build a portfolio of individual companies, but there's a far greater risk of permanent loss of capital. You can also aim to build wealth fast, but this usually means taking more risk — either by chasing longer odds or increasing the size of your bets.

*Big upside, big downside.*

As you can see, risk is not a single event but a hierarchy. You can build wealth steadily but safely while adopting low-risk positions. ETFs can be traded daily on the stock market, which usually gives them good liquidity. On the other hand, any one company can blow up and kill your investment. An index or sector or country could sustain a permanent loss of capital, but it's rare.

You also have the advantage of being able to apply more funds as the investment declines if you are confident that it won't blow up. Again, the focus is on survival, and under conditions of randomness, you will probably bounce back. Big companies with a long history can still blow up, but it's less likely than with younger and newer companies with a shorter track record.

Large companies with many employees are sometimes not allowed by governments to go broke, and so they can be great invest-ments if the price is low in relation to their earnings. But still, they entail a greater risk than country indexes or sectors. This is where our other timeless principles of asset allocation and rebalancing earn their keep. Many investors don't apply these critical principles cor-rectly (or at all).

A losing investment can be a winning investment if you have enough funds and patience and the understanding about normal distributions. If investing is primarily about survival, how do you optimise your bet given the probabilities?

## The risk hierarchy in action

How can you determine what your level of risk is if you know very little about the game (in this case the stock market, its history, its ebbs and flows etc.)? It's misleading to characterise someone's risk level if it changes as the stock market changes.

It can only be based on feeling. Imagine if you knew a lot about the stock market. You would probably agree that there is less risk, and you would buy low and sell high, rather than leave it to an advisor to tell you what to do. Imagine you're playing blackjack. You are dealt two cards. You look at them. *You have an ace and a 9.*

How much do you think you will bet? Now, the dealer deals two cards face up.

*It's 18.* If you know the rules, you might decide to bet a lot. And that would be a great idea. But the reason why you would bet a lot is because you know something about blackjack. If you knew absolutely nothing, then you are just looking at two pieces of thin cardboard with colourful drawings on them. Since a lot of people know very little about markets, they are recommended index funds.

Even the great Warren Buffett says most people should just index if they know nothing.

And if you know very little about the stock market, then it is probably a good idea. The belief is that if you 'know' more about, say, a company, then you can invest with more confidence. But the reality is somewhat different. Just because it is a company you know something about, that doesn't necessarily mean there is less risk (because price is important, and the future is inherently uncertain).

How much do you need to know?

It's only after someone explains the rules of the game to you that you can get a handle on your risk. People get into trouble when they don't know the rules and then increase their risk because they have made money.

> As the old saying goes, any fool can
> make money in a bull market.

The problem is that as the bull market progresses, people bet more and more thereby increasing their risk, while not understanding that this is what's happening. And this happens all the time. Our point is that your risk tolerance is based upon your knowledge levels of yourself as an investor: your understanding of the market, your understanding of social decision-making processes, and what's happening in a market that you are unable to influence.

Again, risk is not static. It changes, as does your risk profile. Most people have an inverted approach to risk, and so at the top, they're pouring more money in (or, even worse, borrowing to fund holidays or house extensions because asset values have increased).

Then instead of taking risk off the table, they despair as the decline happens and then at the bottom cave into the relentless emotional trauma of watching money being lost. So how much do you need to know in order to succeed without raising your risk level? You need to look at history, at least to give you some sort of lower and upper boundary of returns and volatility.

As the old saying goes history doesn't repeat, but it rhymes. You need to look at some statistics. You need an asset allocation — which means keeping some cash spare in case you are wrong or early, and as a safety buffer.

And you need rebalancing — to take advantage of the opportunities for profits.

Nassim Nicholas Taleb says we should look for asymmetrical bets, where the potential upside is unlimited, but the downside is limited[1].

It's what we should do in business, and in life, and it's also what we should be doing as investors.

## How we perceive risk

Let's think about how we normally perceive risk. We see it as having three parts. Firstly, there is your personal financial position. If you are a millionaire and 'risk' $100, then you won't be too concerned as it matters little to your overall wealth. However, if you outlaid $500,000 on an investment, then there's a greater risk since a negative result will impact you considerably more than a $100 loss.

Risk, in order to be useful in investing, must therefore have a context to it. Now, risk can also be approached from the point of your personality as we discussed earlier. We know that we are all not rational investors, and so our personalities play a significant role in how you view risk.

*There are some folks who just don't like any risk, while others are quite comfortable taking higher risk for the potentially higher rewards.*

Knowing your financial position and your personality are critical factors to risk. A third element in assessing risk is having knowledge about the subject matter. The trick is knowing what knowledge or information is important, and whether it contributes to reducing your risk while assisting your returns. Therefore, we believe that if you get the big picture (market cycles) right, then you stand a better than average chance of generating solid investment returns over your investing lifetime.

Just simply knowing about market cycles can improve your investment risk and returns.

## The risk hierarchy: benchmarks

Investing is all about outlaying money today with a plan to get more back in the future, however short or distant that future may be. When we speak of risk, we are really talking about possible future outcomes. When we talk about risk, we must consider the range of options available to us. It's generally agreed that cash is safe but has low returns. Bonds are usually next with stocks being able to, in most cases, deliver over the longer-term higher investment returns.

*Bonds are usually the benchmark.*

For example, if a 10-year government bond paid 4% annually, then you would want stocks to have a larger return, say 8%, given that bonds are very safe, and stocks have a chance of capital loss. When it comes to stocks, there has been traditionally been a strong preference for selecting individual companies rather than investing in sectors or country indexes (or investment *styles* such as value and growth). Alternative choices now exist, and ETFs make investing much easier for those of us who want to manage our own investments.

Part of the reason why individual stocks are favoured is that the finance industry is built for the purpose of generating fees, and so the justification for fees comes from so-called expertise in stock picking, which is supposed to deliver better than average returns.

> *After all, you would hardly pay fees if all the manager did was put your money into an index fund or ETF, which you could quite easily do yourself.*

Paying a fee for performance could be justified if there was solid evidence that managers do add value. However, the evidence shows that most stock pickers and money managers fail to beat the overall index over time. Few have a long-term track record of beating the average.

We develop our portfolio on the belief that understanding a few simple principles and the risk hierarchy can provide solid investment returns over the long term. With regards to knowledge, there is an assumption that if you know a bit about a certain company then you can invest with more confidence. But the reality and the evidence show a somewhat different picture.

Just because it is a company you know something about doesn't mean there is less risk, nor does it mean the investment will generate a better than average return. We're not saying specific knowledge isn't important, and we are strong believers in knowing about the subject matter at hand. That is why we have an overarching philosophy about investing and the 8 timeless principles.

But a critical question is: specifically what knowledge is important, and does it contribute to better returns for the effort expended? How much do you need to know to succeed without raising your risk level?

## Risk defined

We already know that academic papers have tended to define risk as price volatility. The finance industry believes that greater price volatility equates to greater risk. Remember, though, we've never seen anyone complain about volatility when markets are rising!

*Volatility is not the same thing as risk.*

Now if you invest in individual companies, there is always some risk of a permanent loss of capital. The average lifespan of listed companies throughout history is surprisingly short. It could be a dangerous assumption to think that companies will exist for an extended period. Capitalism and competition play their part in killing off the weak (or unlucky) and allowing the strong (or lucky) to survive. As this graphic below shows, most companies are relatively unsuccessful and fail to perform as investments over the long run.

**FIGURE 10.4 – LIFESPAN OF COMPANIES**

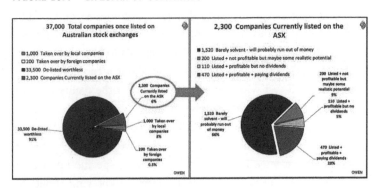

Source: Cuffelinks

When you look at this, you should see two things. One, it is very hard to pick a single company that will be a solid investment over any extended period. While some may profess to have some expertise, the odds are rather stacked against them. When you think about buy-and-hold as an investment philosophy, the previous pie chart gives you plenty of thinking material about why buy-and-hold is not a smart enough investment strategy for the long term.

Therefore, the buying and holding of any single investment is difficult.

Secondly, if you are a long-term investor with a 30-year investing period, you see that in order to beat the average, you would need to select a very high portion of individual winners from a market where there are very few outstanding companies. Remember for a business that becomes insolvent or goes bust, the stock price may hit zero, and there is no coming back from that point.

> *The capital you invest in such a company*
> *is permanently lost.*

There will be no mean reversion. There are also many zombie companies that remain in business but struggle to ever produce a decent investment return.

## ETFs and the risk hierarchy

Buffett says that if you don't know what you are doing, buy an index, because buying an index reduces the risk of losing your money in contrast to trying to pick a series of winners. We agree with that for the know-nothing investor this is sound advice. But we can also take this nugget and tweak it a little. We think that with a small amount of effort and attention, you can generate substantial investment returns with low risk.

We use the risk hierarchy, which involves using ETFs to buy sectors, countries (both developed and emerging), and investing styles (value and growth) when they are cheap, which can generate strong returns without the need to invest in individual companies where the odds of success are relatively lower.

*There is a substantial body of evidence that buying sectors, countries and styles using our 8 Timeless Principles can deliver excellent returns that outperform over the long term.*

Asset allocation and rebalancing play a role, but we want to show in this chapter that there's no need to search for individual companies, read a myriad of annual reports, and possess excellent predictive capacities in order to be a successful investor. You can employ the risk hierarchy along with the principles to deliver consistently solid returns. Buying a diversified product is one of the ways to avoid blowing up your investment account. We'll also show you how to minimise the chances of blowing up by using the principles of asset allocation and rebalancing.

## Countries

Countries seldom go broke. Robert Shiller shows in his book *Irrational Exuberance* shows that countries that have good five-year returns usually do not perform as well over the next five years. The same applies to those countries that have a good one-year return. Now, what we do is focus not on the annual winners but the most recent *losers* and apply the principle of mean reversion.

As is often the case, and the evidence supports the idea that if you buy the 'losing' countries, there is a high probability that they will outperform over the coming 12 to 24 months. When combined with a longer-term macro indicator like the CAPE ratio, you can see excellent returns over even longer periods.

## Sectors

You can apply the same methodology to sectors. Sectors fall in and out of favour too. Look at the quilt graphic and focus not on the winners, but the losing sectors. Buying the losers at the start of the year sees excellent expected future returns.

## FIGURE 10.5 – SECTOR PERFORMANCE

| Abbr | Sector Index | Annual | Best | Worst |
|---|---|---|---|---|
| COND | S&P 500 Consumer Discretionary Index | 11.21% | 43.1% | -33.5% |
| CONS | S&P 500 Consumer Staples Index | 10.08% | 27.6% | -15.4% |
| ENRS | S&P 500 Energy Index | 2.51% | 34.4% | -34.9% |
| FINL | S&P 500 Financials Index | 2.36% | 35.0% | -55.3% |
| HLTH | S&P 500 Health Care Index | 11.08% | 41.5% | -22.8% |
| INDU | S&P 500 Industrials Index | 8.46% | 40.7% | -39.9% |
| INFT | S&P 500 Information Technology Index | 13.79% | 61.7% | -43.1% |
| MATR | S&P 500 Materials Index | 6.86% | 48.6% | -45.7% |
| REAL | S&P 500 Real Estate Index | 5.98% | 32.3% | -42.3% |
| TELS | S&P 500 Communication Services Index | 5.99% | 32.7% | -30.5% |
| UTIL | S&P 500 Utilities Index | 8.53% | 29.0% | -29.0% |
| S&P | S&P 500 Index | 8.81% | 32.4% | -37.0% |

Past performance does not guarantee future returns. The historical performance is meant to show changes in market trends across the different S&P 500 sectors over the past ten years. Returns represent total annual returns (reinvestment of all distributions) and does not include fees and expenses. The investments you choose should reflect your financial goals and risk tolerance. For assistance, talk to a financial professional. All data are as of 12/31/19.

The same approach can be applied to investing styles, value and growth, and even market cap ETFs such as small-, mid-, and large-cap value and growth. To conclude this chapter, we don't deny there are some exceptional investors out there who can deliver great performances by selecting individual company stocks. But relatively few can do this consistently, and there are very few managers you pay fees to who can do this as well.

What we have instead shown you is that you can deliver solid returns using ETFs with significantly reduced risk.

# CHAPTER 11

# PRINCIPLE #5: ASSET ALLOCATION

## Action principles primer

Now that we've covered the four *thought* principles, it's a good time for a brief explainer and recap here regarding the way that our investment approach works. We believe that a successful investment strategy is made up of a few key elements. Firstly, an overarching philosophy helps you to think about how to succeed in all your investments, whether they're in property, stock markets, bonds or any other asset class.

And of course, you then need a set of principles that can be applied in low or high interest rate environments. In our experience, economic conditions change, but we can too easily get caught up in thinking that what is happening now will be with us always. It's a human character trait: when things in the economy and markets are going well, we think that the good times will continue forever. And when things are going badly … we think the same thing.

Neither situation proves to be the case over time.

*It's therefore important that your investment philosophy contains a set of principles that can be applied to any asset class at any time.*

And all decision-making has two parts. The first part involves *thinking* about investing in a philosophical manner or a way that makes sense. These are the four *thought principles*. Put simply, once you decide to start investing in the stock market you should think about risk, your personal financial position, your personality, and timeframes.

The second part comprises the actual actions you take after the decision has been made.

We see this as having four elements, and these are the four *action principles:*

**1.** Asset allocation — how should I allocate my funds across the set of investment opportunities?
**2.** Diversification — am I sufficiently diversified across my asset classes?
**3.** Buy low, sell high — how do I make certain that I am buying low and selling high?
**4.** Rebalancing — do I have a rebalancing plan that allows me to actively manage my individual stocks and my overall portfolio to manage risk?

The four chapters that follow are the *action* principles. They are designed to give you a framework for how to buy and sell stocks.

## Smart allocation

The legendary football player and then coach Knute Rockne once said:

> 'As a coach, I play not my 11 best,
> but my best 11.'

This is also how you should think about your portfolio. Even if equities are the best performing asset class over the long term, your timing is still important. Closer to home, astute asset allocation is aptly demonstrated by Australian residential property in Sydney and Melbourne booming while the ASX meandered back and forth.

Steve:

*I changed jobs around 2000 and started to look for a residential property to live in.*

*Not having a great deal of knowledge about asset classes and property, I bought on the recommendation of a close friend. She lived in the area and the apartment was modern, had city views and was within my budget. I lived in the property for approximately 5 years until I sold it to move to Japan. The property cost me $175,000 and sold it for $326,000 (which was a lot of money back then!).*

*I was delighted to have made a decent sum of money on the property in such a short period of time. When I told people, they assumed that I knew about property and the asset class. In fact I didn't know much at all about property at all. The point was that I made a good return on my "investment" (which is not why I bought it) because I was fortunate enough to be in the right asset class at the right time.*

No genius, just blind luck … and being in the right asset class at the right time.

## The purpose of allocation

Asset allocation can help to deliver smoother risk-adjusted returns to a portfolio. So instead of being all-in on stocks, you spread your funds over, say, property, stocks and cash. It's generally assumed that there is a low correlation between the asset classes, and so their individual performance does not impact on the other classes.

However, because of increasing globalisation over the past 30 years or so, certain asset classes may have increased in their correlation, so it may not be quite as simple as it used to be. Asset allocation is an important investment principle that we use to minimise risk and maximise our investment returns.

# FIGURE 11.1 – ANNUAL RETURNS FOR KEY INDICES (1984 TO 2003)

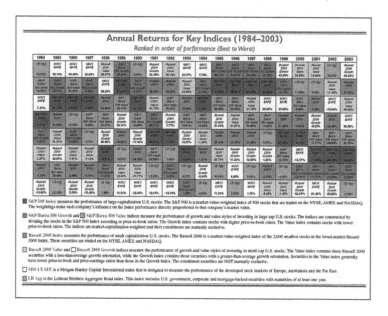

Notice in figure 11.1 how all the asset classes fluctuate.

*We believe the reason why many investors underperform is that they make some basic errors in their asset allocation.*

While diversification is a sensible principle, we also believe that a solid asset allocation strategy will improve your investment returns. Firstly, let us state that there is no single correct way to allocate. It's not an exact science.

What you will most likely find is that you wished you had put more into the winner and less into the loser, regardless of how carefully you planned an investment strategy. Hindsight bias is a wonderful thing!

But we're all about growing our wealth sensibly, and that means taking an evidence-based approach.

## Asset allocation in action

We think of asset allocation in *two* ways — macro asset allocation and micro asset allocation.

### Macro allocation

This is straightforward. It simply means dividing your funds between your chosen asset classes, and partly because of tax incentives in Australia this allocation is normally dominated by stocks and property. We can also include cash and bonds as they can be useful asset classes for protecting capital.

Since we understand market cycles, we believe there is ample evidence to show that moving between asset classes at the macro level can increase your returns. For example, as Steve experienced above, he made excellent investment returns simply by choosing property when it was on the cusp of a large increase. The same can be done for stocks using market cycles and the CAPE ratio.

*With the advent of ETFs, which allow us to buy country indexes, US sectors, and styles, we can use the cycles to increase our returns.*

When stocks are cheap, you should consider allocating more of your funds to stocks in order to gains the increased returns on offer. When stocks are expensive and offering minimal or below-average returns, then you should pivot to alternative asset classes such as property or cash.

Remember, cash has an important role to play because it's uncorrelated with stocks, it gives you a safety buffer, and it gives you the *optionality* to buy stocks when they do become cheap. There is no 'correct' allocation as it depends on your personality, finances, and available options, but again if you understand market cycles, you should adapt your allocation accordingly.

## Micro allocation

Micro allocation is how we divide our funds once we have determined our macro allocation. An example will suffice. Let's use US sector ETFs, where we might be looking to invest in the most out of favour sectors. At the time of writing, we have no way of knowing for sure how this will play out. But if history is any guide, then energy, materials, industrials, financials and communications look to be worthy of consideration due to being out of favour.

Then we would go on to look at the CAPE ratio for each sector. In this case, at the end of 2018, the US market is expensive, so some caution is warranted.

## FIGURE 11.2 – SECTOR PERFORMANCE

### S&P 500 Sector Performance

| 2007 | 2008 | 2009 | 2010 | 2011 | 2012 | 2013 | 2014 | 2015 | 2016 | 2017 | 2018 |
|---|---|---|---|---|---|---|---|---|---|---|---|
| ENRS 34.4% | CONS -15.4% | INFT 61.7% | REAL 32.3% | UTIL 19.9% | FINL 28.8% | COND 43.1% | REAL 30.2% | COND 10.1% | ENRS 27.4% | INFT 38.8% | HLTH 6.5% |
| MATR 22.5% | HLTH -22.8% | MATR 48.6% | COND 27.7% | CONS 14.0% | COND 23.9% | HLTH 41.5% | UTIL 29.0% | HLTH 6.9% | TELS 23.5% | MATR 23.8% | UTIL 4.1% |
| UTIL 19.4% | UTIL -29.0% | COND 41.3% | INDU 26.7% | HLTH 12.7% | REAL 19.7% | INDU 40.7% | HLTH 25.3% | CONS 6.6% | FINL 22.8% | COND 23.0% | COND 0.8% |
| INFT 16.3% | TELS -30.5% | REAL 27.1% | MATR 22.2% | REAL 11.4% | TELS 18.3% | FINL 35.6% | INFT 20.1% | INFT 5.9% | INDU 18.9% | FINL 22.2% | INFT -0.3% |
| CONS 14.2% | COND -33.5% | S&P 26.5% | ENRS 20.5% | TELS 8.3% | HLTH 18.2% | S&P 32.4% | CONS 16.0% | REAL 4.7% | MATR 16.7% | HLTH 22.1% | REAL -2.2% |
| INDU 12.0% | ENRS -34.9% | INDU 20.9% | TELS 19.0% | COND 6.1% | S&P 16.0% | INFT 28.4% | FINL 15.2% | TELS 3.4% | UTIL 16.3% | S&P 21.8% | S&P -4.4% |
| TELS 11.9% | S&P -37.0% | HLTH 19.7% | S&P 15.1% | ENRS 4.7% | INDU 15.4% | CONS 26.1% | S&P 13.7% | S&P 1.4% | INFT 13.9% | INDU 21.0% | CONS -8.4% |
| HLTH 7.2% | INDU -39.9% | FINL 17.2% | CONS 14.1% | INFT 2.4% | MATR 15.0% | MATR 25.6% | INDU 9.8% | FINL 12.0% | S&P 12.0% | CONS 13.5% | TELS -12.5% |
| S&P 5.5% | REAL -42.3% | CONS 14.9% | FINL 12.1% | S&P 2.1% | INFT 14.8% | ENRS 25.1% | COND 9.7% | INDU -2.5% | COND 6.0% | UTIL 12.1% | FINL -13.0% |
| COND -13.2% | INFT -43.1% | ENRS 13.8% | INFT 10.2% | INDU -0.5% | CONS 10.8% | UTIL 13.2% | MATR 6.9% | UTIL -4.8% | CONS 5.4% | REAL 10.9% | INDU -13.2% |
| REAL -17.9% | MATR -45.7% | UTIL 11.9% | UTIL 5.5% | MATR -9.6% | ENRS 4.6% | TELS 11.5% | TELS 3.0% | MATR -8.4% | REAL 3.4% | ENRS -1.0% | MATR -14.7% |
| FINL -18.6% | FINL -55.3% | TELS 8.9% | HLTH 2.9% | FINL -17.1% | UTIL 1.3% | REAL 1.6% | ENRS -7.8% | ENRS -21.1% | HLTH -2.7% | TELS -1.3% | ENRS -18.1% |

| Abbr. | Sector Index | Annual | Best | Worst |
|---|---|---|---|---|
| COND | S&P 500 Consumer Discretionary Index | 9.92% | 43.1% | -33.5% |
| CONS | S&P 500 Consumer Staples Index | 8.73% | 26.1% | -15.4% |
| ENRS | S&P 500 Energy Index | 1.78% | 34.4% | -34.9% |
| FINL | S&P 500 Financials Index | 0.21% | 35.6% | -55.3% |
| HLTH | S&P 500 Health Care Index | 10.31% | 41.5% | -22.6% |
| INDU | S&P 500 Industrials Index | 6.88% | 40.7% | -39.9% |
| INFT | S&P 500 Information Technology Index | 11.18% | 61.7% | -43.1% |
| MATR | S&P 500 Materials Index | 5.51% | 48.6% | -45.7% |
| REAL | S&P 500 Real Estate Index | 4.26% | 32.3% | -42.3% |
| TELS | S&P 500 Communication Services Index | 4.02% | 23.5% | -30.5% |
| UTIL | S&P 500 Utilities Index | 7.16% | 29.0% | -29.0% |
| S&P | S&P 500 Index | 7.11% | 32.4% | -37.0% |

Past performance does not guarantee future returns. The historical performance is meant to show changes in market trends across the different S&P 500 sectors over the past ten years. Returns represent total annual returns (reinvestment of all distributions) and does not include fees and expenses. The investments you choose should reflect your financial goals and risk tolerance. For assistance, talk to a financial professional. All data are as of 12/31/18.

Source: Novel Investor

You may choose three methods to invest:

1. Invest in all the out of favour sectors equally because while some investments will seem more appealing and appear to have more potential, you can't always be sure; or
2. Invest in all sectors but adjust the initial amounts according to some indicator (you may choose a greater weighting based on market cycles and where the sector performs best in through the business cycle); or
3. A judgemental selection of sectors — we believe this is a sound approach as it allows you to adjust your allocation according to our 8 timeless principles (for example, mean reversion and CAPE ratios).

Under this method, you would select those sectors that have the best expected returns (we favour buying the bottom three performers ('the losers'), and then allowing mean reversion to play its role in delivering solid investment returns.

Notice how over an extended period that no one sector dominates, and so they swap positions. Leaders become laggards, and vice versa. You can weight your initial allocation as follows:

Say the energy sector as at 31 December is the underperformer over the previous 12 months and at the bottom of the list.

As such, you can expect mean reversion to kick in, but you cannot be too sure when this will happen.

This is where the micro allocation becomes important.

*Many investors over-allocate or allocate the full 100% of funds rather than keeping some cash allocated against the stock.*

This is often done because you think the opportunity is so good. So many folks leave themselves no wriggle room or opportunity to buy after their initial allocation. However, it is more prudent if you choose $10,000 as your potential allocation, to initially spend $5,000 and hold $5,000 against it in cash.

After all, none of us is clairvoyant — we can't pick the bottom of the market accurately — and so it pays to keep some of your powder dry in case the price sinks lower. This can often be the case because you are buying when the sector or country is out of favour — but remember that is when the best returns are on offer.

You can repeat this strategy (buy low, sell high) on an annual basis. Simply check the bottom three performers and allocate your funds accordingly. Now in the example above, the bottom three sectors in 2018 are quite likely to bounce back in 2019.

But the opportunities aren't that compelling because the CAPE ratios are still high.

**Now if the sector is at the bottom *and* it has a lower than average CAPE ratio, then this is a more compelling scenario — and you could start with, say, $7,000 in the stock and $3,000 in cash.**

Again there is no 'correct' formula, but where the expected returns are high, you should consider starting with a higher initial allocation. Now we expect some to say: *'Well, that's a lot of cash to be holding and it's not earning much in this low interest rate environment, so …'*

Thus, let's talk about cash and why it is so valuable.

## Cash is *(sometimes)* king!

Cash is important for several reasons. Firstly, cash gives you options. As Warren Buffett said, holding cash is painful but a lot less painful than making a dumb investment decision and losing money. Although we cannot predict what future opportunities may arise, cash allows you to take advantage of them when they do.

If you are investing systematically, then you should be piling up cash as the market rises and utilising additional cash when the market is falling. Investing over cycles means taking a dynamic approach, and we discuss that more in the principle of rebalancing. That is how investors end up with a better than average return over the long term.

For those of you thinking, *'Gosh, maybe I have a dud investment, so more funds might not be a great idea'*.

OK, we hear you. But given we are using ETFs, there's a very low probability that the asset classes (such as sectors, countries or styles) will stay low forever (see again the chapters on mean reversion and risk hierarchy).

> *Secondly, having cash against each stock allows you to add additional funds if the stock falls.*

We've found this to be very reassuring psychologically. Firstly, we have the knowledge and emotional comfort of having cash available should the stock price fall, and so we can put our cash to work and realise that we are reducing our average entry price as the stock falls.

This leads on to the second point. Over time you will find that holding cash (which does at least earn a small amount of interest) helps you to outperform the market. Another reason for appropriate asset allocation is that markets fluctuate. Have a look at the intra-year fluctuations of Australia's ASX 200 index in figure 11.3.

**FIGURE 11.3 – ASX INTRA-YEAR DECLINES VS. CALENDAR YEAR RETURNS**

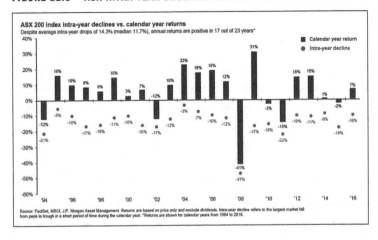

And here is the US market intra-year volatility in figure 11.4 below.

**FIGURE 11.4 – S&P 500 VOLATILITY**

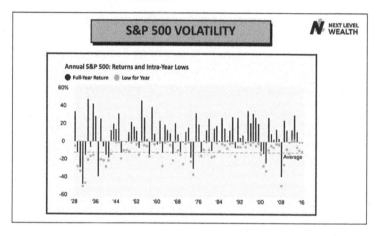

In short, markets can be volatile! And this volatility can be your friend because it throws up opportunities. Holding spare cash gives you a greater range of options to add more stocks during those intra-year declines. Stock markets can fall 20% to 40% in a very short space of time, and if you have cash, you can take advantage of these falls. Even better, when the CAPE ratio is low — and by now we hope you are realising what type of market and where in the cycle you are presently — is important for asset allocation.

Secondly, you can adjust your asset allocation according to the expected return.

*Expected returns are not an exact science, but in general, we know that when the expected return is high, you should consider increasing your initial allocation.*

So if the expected return is high (as happens when asset classes are cheap and out of favour), then you may start with a 70% allocation and hold 30% in cash. We will see in our chapter on the buy low, sell high principle why this is a good strategy. Remember Warren Buffett's number one rule is:

*'Don't lose money.'*

Having a set of investment principles that include a disciplined approach to asset allocation will certainly increase the probability that your investments will adhere to Buffett's number one rule.

# CHAPTER 12

# PRINCIPLE #6: BUY LOW, SELL HIGH!

## The swinging moods of Mr Market

Buy low, sell high is one of those principles that just sounds too easy. But there are two important components of successfully buying low and selling high. The first is that you must often *wait* for the opportunities to arrive. Successful investing depends upon waiting and then taking advantage of the investment opportunities offered.

The second component is *acting* when the time comes. In order to make above-average returns, you must be able to pull the trigger when the time comes. Again, this sounds easy, but the outstanding returns are made by buying low, and doing this usually comes at times of great turmoil and doubt.

Ben Graham described a character he called Mr Market in his remarkable book *The Intelligent Investor*[1] Imagine for a moment that you're the owner of a thriving business, whatever that business may be. And now let's imagine there's a man who has a serious mood disorder, who we'll choose to call 'Mr Market'.

Mr Market is a highly temperamental and emotional fellow … and he suffers from extremes in mood swings! Each day Mr Market will toddle over and offer to buy your business at a certain price. Some days Mr Market may be in a jolly good mood, and when this is so, he may offer you a high price for your business.

On darker days, however, Mr Market may seem to be rather depressed … and on such days he may offer only a very low price for your business. Your business may be successful throughout the whole period — this may not change from week to week or from month to month — only the mood of Mr Market changes.

> *Of course, you should not sell your thriving business to Mr Market at a low price just because Mr Market may be in a bad mood.*

Now perhaps you *could* decide to sell to Mr Market if he's feeling a little exuberant and the price is high enough. Simplified though this analogy is, this dynamic is what faces investors in the stock market. The stock market quotes prices on all sorts of businesses every single day, and the price quoted can vary wildly depending on the prevailing mood. To be a successful investor, you need to be able to do one thing consistently, and that is to …

## Buy low and sell high!

In a previous chapter of the book, we discussed mean reversion. To implement and take advantage of mean reversion, you must be able to, as the saying goes buy low, sell high (BLSH). Like many investment principles, it's simple but not easy.

The 'not easy' part is because our own emotions, like those of Mr Market, play such a dominant role in determining our investment approach. It's easy in a cool and calm situation to say that you will BLSH, but in the heat of the moment when it comes to buying or selling, many investors hesitate, allowing their emotions to take over their investment strategy.

> *And so the principle of buy low, sell high is one that does not come naturally to most investors.*

We tend to live mostly in the moment or the recent past, so we assume that what happened last week, last month, will continue to happen in the foreseeable future. Sometimes this is the case, but it's not necessarily correct over the longer term.

This is because there are two major timeframes in markets — momentum in the short term, and mean reversion over the medium-to-longer term. As Ben Graham also said, in the short term the stock market is voting machine — meaning in the short term what's popular gets more popular, and what's hated gets more hated — but over the long run, it's a weighing machine.

We've discussed mean reversion and how this plays a central role in our strategy to buy low and sell high. We would be the first to admit it is not always easy to do, and it is difficult to look at a stock or index that has fallen 50% or more over the recent past and decide that it is a good investment for the future.

We just naturally project the past into the future. But over the long term mean reversion does take place. Stocks mean revert. The popular ones start falling, and the hated ones start rising. And so if we know this then BLSH becomes a little easier, especially if we can maintain our disciplined systematic approach.

> *Put simply, that means buy low and sell high.*

To get above-average returns in a dynamic system, you should start out below average. As John Templeton said:

> *'It is impossible to produce a superior performance unless you do something different from the majority.'*

So what can we do that is 'different from the majority'? We can buy BLSH, and we can show you how it works as there's plenty of evidence. Have a look at the following:

## FIGURE 12.1 – WHAT HAPPENS WHEN YOU BUY ASSETS DOWN 80%?

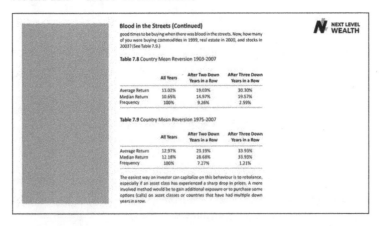

BUY LOW SELL HIGH

**NEXT LEVEL WEALTH**

### What Happens When You Buy Assets Down 80%

We've done a lot of articles on value and drawdowns on the blog before (search the archives). I was curious what happens when you bought the US equity sectors back when they were really hammered (French Fama to 1920s).

Average 3 year nominal returns when buying a sector down since 1920s:

60% = 57%
70% = 87%
80% = 172%
90% = 240%

Average 3 year nominal returns when buying an industry down since 1920s:

60% = 71%
70% = 96%
80% = 136%
90% = 115%

Average 8 year nominal returns when buying a country down since 1970s:

60% = 107%
70% = 116%
80% = 118%
90% = 156%

It's hard to buy something down 80%, especially if you owned it when it was down 30, 50, then 80%

Source: Meb Faber

Notice how buying cheaply delivers outsized returns. It happens to stocks, sectors, industries, countries, and investment styles.

## FIGURE 12.2 – BLOOD ON THE STREETS

**Blood in the Streets (Continued)**

**NEXT LEVEL WEALTH**

good times to be buying when there was blood in the streets. Now, how many of you were buying commodities in 1999, real estate in 2000, and stocks in 2003? (See Table 7.9.)

**Table 7.8** Country Mean Reversion 1903-2007

|  | All Years | After Two Down Years in a Row | After Three Down Years in a Row |
|---|---|---|---|
| Average Return | 13.02% | 19.03% | 30.30% |
| Median Return | 10.65% | 14.97% | 19.57% |
| Frequency | 100% | 9.26% | 2.59% |

**Table 7.9** Country Mean Reversion 1975-2007

|  | All Years | After Two Down Years in a Row | After Three Down Years in a Row |
|---|---|---|---|
| Average Return | 12.97% | 23.19% | 33.93% |
| Median Return | 12.18% | 28.68% | 33.93% |
| Frequency | 100% | 7.27% | 1.21% |

The easiest way an investor can capitalize on this behaviour is to rebalance, especially if an asset class has experienced a sharp drop in prices. A more involved method would be to gain additional exposure or to purchase some options (calls) on asset classes or countries that have had multiple down years in a row.

Now look at those returns and try to tell us that buying low is 'risky'! So BLSH can deliver you above-average returns. The alternative is you can try every year or two to choose the specific stocks, managed funds, or ETFs that will outperform.

But the evidence shows that this is a very hard task even for the 'experts' and professionals. And there's also the role of luck to be considered as well. If mean reversion happens to indexes and ETFs, then it makes more sense to BLSH than try and get lucky for a large portion of the time.

### Note we said buy low *AND* sell high.

In order to maximise your returns, you must do both. Let's break this down. It means you should dispense with the idea that you are a 'buy-and-hold' investor. You are simply an investor.

A corollary of this is that you also need to dispense with the idea of yourself as a long-term holder of stocks. Yes, even most of the winning stocks must be sold when they're no longer cheap. And finally, contrary to what many say, it *is* possible to time the market. You'll hear many financial people mention *Buffett* and *buy* and *long* in the same sentence. But those who think Buffett is not a market timer are wrong. Buffett is a value investor and he purchases most stock when markets crash.

### This is market timing!

The economy has business cycles, and there's no reason that your investment strategy should not cycle as well. Buffett adopted this approach from Ben Graham, his mentor who also spoke of the advantages of buying stocks when the whole market is low. Remember the CAPE ratio tells us when markets are favourably disposed to higher expected returns. Momentum and mean reversion happen because many investors follow the price rather than the value and let their emotions play a role in investing.

As we have been at pains to point out, a systematic approach will beat an emotional approach every time. You raise your probability of success if you patiently wait for cheap markets to invest more. And, paraphrasing James Montier, if you don't buy stocks when they are cheap then when do you buy them?[2] If the table above doesn't get you thinking about buying low, then nothing will.

Many financial folks tell you not to 'time the market' or derivations of this theme. Or 'be a long-term investor'. The fact is that, on average, you are better off selling after a good return and looking for the next bargain. This way your money will compound faster.

So far we've expended more words on buying low than selling.

Why? As Charlie Munger, Buffett's long-time business partner says:

> *'A stock well bought is half sold.'*

Combined with our other principles like asset allocation and rebalancing, you can see the logic and power of BLSH. So when do you sell? What's a good return? Well, have a look at the chart below.

**FIGURE 12.3 – TIME, DIVERSIFICATION AND VOLATILITY OF RETURNS**

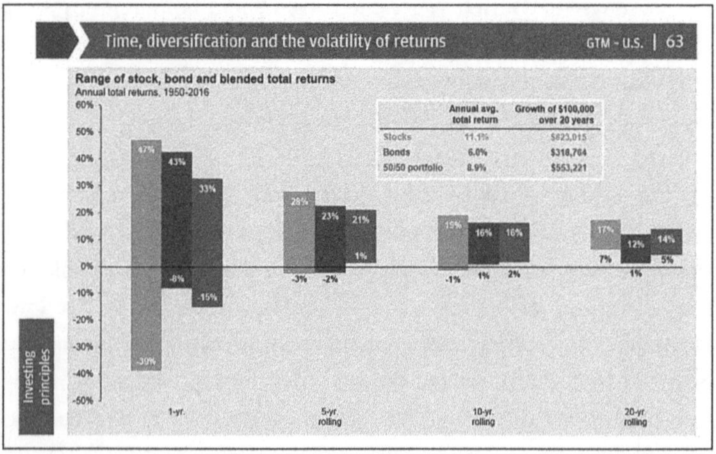

Source: JP Morgan

Note how after 12 months, that the returns start to decline and end up at the long-term average. This makes sense because if you know stocks return 8–10% over the long term (really it is perhaps closer to 6% compounding, less inflation), then the longer you hold, the greater the probability that the long-term average is exactly the return you will get.

So take profits and avoid a cardinal sin of many investors — getting greedy.

## Buy low, sell high in action

So the first aspect of BLSH is considering the level of the relevant market overall. As Ben Stein points out in his excellent book *Yes, You Can Time the Market*:

> *'People come to accept the notion that the price of the market was irrelevant when price was so ruthlessly applied elsewhere.'*

So in your search for promising investments, look for markets, sectors or styles that are out of favour. There will be plenty of bad news and pessimistic forecasts, but you must start here in order to achieve the above-average returns.

Thanks to the advent of ETFs, you can buy the country indexes and sectors, or if you like individual companies, you can search for 52-week lows or stocks with low P/E ratios for potential candidates.

We think country and sector investments are better for most investors given our risk hierarchy, but some folks just like individual companies, and that may be fair enough provided they're mindful of risk and look towards safer companies with an established track record. A cheap stock market usually implies there will be plenty of individual companies within the market that are cheap.

Now, that does not mean you can buy any old company. We tend to aim for large systemic companies with modest debt levels that pay a dividend. We've found that this is a good place to start, especially in a low interest rate environment. Remember there are two parts to this equation — buy and sell — we sell after mean reversion kicks in or at least wait 12 months when the tax implications are positive.

Then repeat the 'buy low' process again.

> *Remember, paper profits are not*
> *realised until you sell.*

Mean reversion should be at the forefront of your mind, so don't get psyched out if the stock falls further. As the old saying goes, you make your money in bear markets, you just don't know it yet. It's nearly always difficult to see mean reversion when things look so miserable, but in most cases, things do change, and they do get better.

BLSH is an important part of our investment success. Don't expect every single investment to be a big winner. This isn't realistic, and there is no one who has a perfect 100% track record of success. Even Warren Buffett picks duds sometimes.

## Applying BLSH through the cycles

Those who take a systematic approach to investing understand that it is nearly impossible to buy low at the exact bottom or sell at exactly the top. Cheap stocks can always get cheaper, and expensive stocks can continue to get more expensive. Remember the more it falls, the more chance there is that at some point soon the stock or ETF will most likely stop falling, and the momentum will swing to mean reversion.

You'll never have perfect timing other than through blind luck. If you use our asset allocation principle you will reduce your probability of running out of cash. Remember it's about having and maintaining a disciplined and systematic approach. It will feel uncomfortable, emotionally, but you now have ample evidence to show that buy BLSH works.

Make sure you take a long-term view and approach (which is different from being a long term buy-and-hold investor) and take profits when your investments start to generate solid returns. Your investments and wealth compound by avoiding the losers.

Remember, then, the importance of asset allocation. It is difficult to get the exact percentage right with each investment, and so we encourage a conservative approach since cheap stocks often become even cheaper in the short term. Holding some cash against an investment gives you the comfort of having the ability to buy more if the stock continues to fall and lower your overall purchase price.

And finally, think like a contrarian. Don't be contrarian just for the sake of it — the crowd can be right some of the time, and this can see your returns diminish if you buy too early in the fall or sell too late. Focus on using the long-term averages such as the CAPE ratio as a guide to determine when to buy low and sell high.

**CHAPTER 13**

# PRINCIPLE #7: DIVERSIFICATION

## All eggs in one basket

There's an old saying that you shouldn't put all of your eggs in one basket. That's because if you drop the basket, all of the eggs might become broken! A similar analogy can be applied to fruit: if you put all of your fruit in one place, one rotten apple can rot and spoil the cart.

Pete:

*When I was growing up, I was obsessed with cricket, and we played until it got dark most summer evenings.*

*At the back of our house was a patio with one massive windowpane, so we weren't supposed to play with the hard cricket ball anywhere near that window.*

*Well, of course, you can guess what happened!*

*I might've tried to explain to Dad that if they'd had lots of smaller windowpanes then perhaps only one of them might've broken, and the cost to replace it might have been much less.*

*I don't think Dad was in much of a mood for that discussion, though, perhaps justifiably!*

Farmers have understood diversification for centuries.

For example, they will know that if their entire harvest comprises one type of produce, then there is a risk that needs to be managed. The risk can be managed by harvesting different types of crop, in different fields, or from locking in some of the gains through hedging or derivatives markets.

## Diversification thoughts

Arguably, diversification is the number one principle that you will hear about from an overwhelming majority of financial advisors or planners. Diversification has been promoted as a standard refrain for a long time as a way to reduce risk in a portfolio. The risk of loss from putting all your funds in just one or two stocks is higher than it is from putting your money into 100 stocks. Hence diversification is the prevailing mantra.

And so most investment portfolios look alike, made up of a residential property, some shares, and a superannuation account (which is usually more weighted towards stocks). Another reason given to diversify is that according to the Efficient Market Hypothesis (EMH), you can't beat the overall market, and so the best approach is to simply buy the index and receive the market return.

In other words, trying to consistently pick companies that will outperform all the other is nigh on impossible, so don't bother. We discussed the related challenges in the risk hierarchy section of the book. Buffett said that diversification is for folks who don't know what they're doing. He's not being rude but simply stating that unless you want to spend a lot of time looking at company balance sheets and the 'fundamentals', you should heed his advice.

Buy an index fund, sit back, and collect the pot when you retire. But the problem for many people is that they won't have enough for retirement, and so you could be excused for asking if just buying an index fund (diversification) is the best approach. Since the early 1980s, though, the world has undergone considerable change.

Pete thinks back to his father's career:

*Dad worked in one career for his entire adult life.*

*He paid off his home, and the financial plan was the pension.*

*A few individuals participated in privatisation stock market floats, but most people didn't invest in shares.*

*And since interest rates were so high, investment property wasn't popular either.*

*In fact, most people struggled to pay off their mortgage debt as quickly as they possibly could!*

Since the 1980s, there has been an increasing linkage between each country's economy as they expand trade in goods and services. As each country connects, their stock markets have also begun to show an increasing correlation. If you look at the graph below, you see that many of the major developed markets move in some kind of sync.

What varies is the level of returns. This is an important consideration point for diversification.

## FIGURE 13.1 – COMPARING MAJOR WORLD INDEXES SINCE 2000

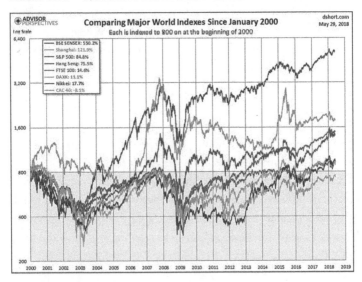

Source: Advisor Perspectives

The primary idea behind diversification, then, is to assist in reducing your risk.

A little money in the US market, a little in Europe, and perhaps some in the emerging markets is an example of how diversification can work in practice. Or at a higher level, some in stocks, some in property, and some in bonds or cash.

## The home bias

When it comes to investing many of us fail to adequately diversify at both levels. The reality is that most of us like to invest in stocks and property that is close to home. Many property investors will invest close to their own suburb, or in their home city.

Some psychological comfort is provided if you can drive past your investment property — people often see property as being somewhat more tangible than stocks. Investment property will often be either close by or just a short flight away. People act in a somewhat similar fashion when it comes to stocks.

Part of the problem with taking a narrow view is that in a low interest rate world there are still many solid investment opportunities overseas, even when they're scarce in our home market.

*In stock markets, investors in most countries —
and Australia is no exception — have what
is called a home bias.*

In figure 13.2 you can see that Australia makes up approximately 2–3% of global stock markets. But we have a very high rate of home bias with many investors choosing to keep their funds in the home market. In this respect, we're not unusual. Over the past 120 years, Australia has actually been the most successful stock market with the highest returns.

But remember that sort of timeframe is not applicable to you as a single investor. Bull and bear markets count! There have been many periods when the Australian market has underperformed overseas markets too. This is why diversification makes sense where you can take advantage of overseas markets that offer potentially higher returns.

When local stock market returns (especially in the low interest rate environment) may look low, overseas markets may still provide opportunities to generate solid investment returns. This is why we take a global approach to investing, in order to generate returns consistently.

**FIGURE 13.2 – THE HOME BIAS**

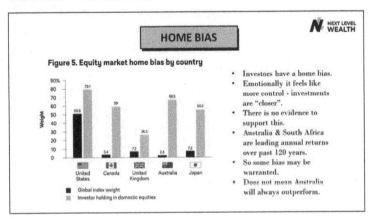

First, you need to shed the psychological comfort of the home market bias and be able to look to overseas markets. This alone makes diversification an important principle in investing. Let's assume that you are convinced to start looking overseas. Now before you rush off, we need to understand the correlation between overseas markets.

The old assumption related to diversification was that the correlation between individual countries is small, and so fluctuations in say the US market would not impact stocks in Europe or emerging markets, such as, say, Brazil. However, since the 1980s and with globalisation, correlations between stock markets have been increasing.

## FIGURE 13.3 – INCREASING CORRELATIONS

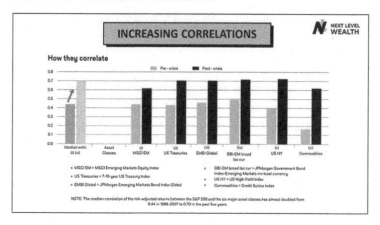

There's a growing need, then, to pay attention to how you are diversified in your stock portfolio. The global financial crisis provided evidence that global markets are more correlated than was previously thought, and so diversification on that occasion did not provide great protection. The big US stock market decline in 2007–08 took down almost every other market with it.

If you look at a quilt of returns from developed markets, you'll notice how markets move in sync with each other to a certain extent. Very often, developed markets will move in unison, though the exact returns will naturally vary. The US market may return a positive, say, 12%, the ASX 25%, and the UK 16%.

We follow the daily movements, and we have noted that around 60% of the time when the US market rises or falls on any given trading day, the ASX usually goes in the same direction the following day. While the annual stock market returns may vary, the same applies to annual returns as well. Most years that the US stock market rises, so too does the ASX in Australia.

It's important to understand the role of the US market in the global context. The US represents approximately 45% of the global stock market. And so what happens there affects all other markets. The old saying is 'if the US sneezes everyone catches a cold'.

And Australia is not immune, although Australia is linked closely with China too these days, due to our resources exports. Matthew Kidman in his book *Bulls, Bears & a Croupier*, discussed what happened in 2007/08:

> '*With the benefit of hindsight, we all now know the Australian share market acted in lockstep with its American contemporary, falling 55% over a 16-month period.*'

As we say, when the poop hits the fan, everything correlates to one! This is an important consideration for diversification. If you're thinking '*Yes, but these events don't happen all that often*', then you should consider again the folks who planned on retiring in 2008. Many found their superannuation had halved as a result of the US market, which many had assumed not to have too much influence on Australia's economy and stock market.

When Buffett suggested those without knowledge or motivation should just invest in index funds and bonds, what he didn't say was spread your funds across asset classes. We discussed our approach to this in the chapter on asset allocation. He said most of us should just index as a way of diversifying.

But for those who know what they're doing or those with a desire to learn and manage their own finances (specialisation through increasing one's knowledge), diversifying within one asset class can build wealth. Buffett is living proof as his obsession with business and stock markets has made him extremely wealthy. Buffett does not diversify broadly, and it doesn't appear to have affected his wealth too much! Most of his funds are in stocks, and he is very heavily invested in only a few stocks.

He simply buys what's cheap in the same asset class as a way to build wealth rather than diversify to the point where returns are eaten away by the 'need' to reduce risk through diversification.

## The Goldilocks portfolio

Imagine this scenario. Your neighbour approaches you with an offer to buy their house at a very cheap price. You know with a high degree of confidence that you could buy and sell it quickly to make a good profit. Or join it to your property and sell the two blocks together.

It would seem rather silly to say: *'Thanks mate, but I'm really into diversification and since I already have a house, another one would increase my investment portfolio risk, so I'll pass.'*

Make sense? What we're really talking about with diversification is how much knowledge you need to build wealth. A portfolio using our investment philosophy and the 8 timeless principles is for investors who don't want to be completely passive in their investment approach (that is, maximising diversification by simply buying an index like the ASX 300 and then holding it forever). We have shown that this buy-and-hold approach doesn't work in all markets.

Using our investment philosophy and the 8 Timeless Principles can give you a degree of diversification sufficient to generate above-average returns in a low interest rate world.

*We think the best approach is to invest globally using the macro valuation methods such as CAPE to point you in the direction of potentially higher returns.*

Yes, there's still a correlation between markets, but generally, the CAPE ratio shows that countries (and indeed individual stocks) that are already cheap do not fall as much as their higher priced compatriots. In a globalised world it is critical to watch what is happening in — and the valuation of — the US market.

It's simply folly to believe that a whale of a market will not impact the large number of minnows. When the US is expensive (as it is of the time of writing), it is prudent to reduce your exposure to markets that may be more expensive than their average CAPE ratio.

You should not, however, avoid all investing because the US is expensive. If you invest in overseas markets by taking a long-term approach, you can purchase large-cap systemic type stocks that pay a reasonable dividend, or you can focus on ETFs and diversify across countries, sectors and styles that are cheap.

Combined with the principle of asset allocation and rebalancing, we can succeed in generating solid returns in a low-interest rate environment, even while the US market is expensive.

When the next US correction comes around, it will bring other developed markets down with it, and you will have some dry powder (cash!) to capitalise on the wonderful opportunities that such corrections always bring.

## CHAPTER 14

# PRINCIPLE #8: REBALANCING

## Keeping a balanced wardrobe

When you buy new clothes, you naturally do so with a view to what's already in your wardrobe. Or, at least, you should! After all, if you have a perfectly good tuxedo hanging up at home and you go clothes shopping, then it doesn't make much sense to go out and buy more tuxedo suits. Now you may find from time to time that you have a shortage of casual shirts, or warm clothes going into the winter months. And if that's the case you look to buy some at a convenient time and price.

Pete:

*Last Christmas, I received three gifts that included new socks. Now that's great, I like receiving new socks — it's a sign of middle age, I guess — but naturally I now don't intend to buy any for some time!*

It's a bit the same when you manage a portfolio of investments.

If one of your investments has done spectacularly well, you may find that your portfolio becomes a little unbalanced.

Now, on the one hand, this might not seem to matter too much.

But remember, we are aiming to create a timeless investment strategy here, that will see you through all markets and all cycles.

Also remember the oldest rule of engineering:

*If something can go wrong, it eventually will.*

That's why balance is important because it doesn't leave you too exposed to any one market or investment position. A bit like me with my sock draw, we need to undertake a periodic rebalancing exercise!

## Taking a profit

Brokers often advise their clients to buy and hold.

*'Focus on the average annual increases in stock prices'* they say.

Or they say:

*'Don't try to time the market, seeking the golden moment to buy or sell.'*

But as we now know, what matters is the actual returns you get on your capital, not the average.

> *Some of the most successful investors are those who did, in fact, get the timing right.*

Suppose some big news has inflated a stock price by 40 per cent in a week, more than twice its normal volatility. What are the odds that, anytime soon, yet another 40 per cent run will occur? Not impossible, of course, but certainly not large.

A prudent investor would do as the Wall Street professionals:

*'Take a profit.'* BENOIT MANDELBROT

## Rebalancing thoughts

The simple quote above is from Benoit Mandelbrot's excellent book *The (Mis)Behavior of Markets*. Rebalancing is an important investment principle and one that is at the core of our portfolio management. The reason why is because investing is most difficult when you let your emotions rule your decision-making process.

And rebalancing is hard because it entails selling a portion of your winners — possibly when you feel they might have further to run — and buying some more of your 'losers' again, when you think they might sink further. How many of us happily take profits from our winners and place that hard-won capital into our 'losers'?

Despite the emotional ickiness (yes, it's a word because we looked it up), we rebalance regularly, and we can tell you that even after managing money for a long time, it is emotionally painful to reduce a position if the investment is up by 50% or more. And it's even more painful to put the profits into an underperforming investment!

However, contrary to your ickiness (OK, we'll stop using it now), studies show that rebalancing on a regular basis outperforms a buy-and-hold portfolio. Many advisors do not discuss the influence that rebalancing can have on investment returns for your portfolio, but rebalancing plays a very significant role in successful investing.

*Studies have shown that the more consistently you rebalance, the better the returns will be over time.*

But we understand that many people don't want to be bothered with rebalancing their portfolio on a daily basis. But even if you don't do it daily, doing it weekly, monthly, quarterly, or even annually will deliver better returns than a simple buy-and-hold strategy.

## What a Turkey!

By way of a real-life example, have a look at Turkey in the chart in figure 14.1 to see how challenging it could be to rebalance in a systematic way. Firstly, note the volatility of the returns, which range from a high of 125.9% in 2003 (thus handing you dinner party bragging rights!) to a gut-wrenching loss of -62.1% in 2008. Now, to be fair, everything got smashed in 2008, but strangely enough, we've never found much comfort in knowing that everybody else got smashed as well!

Had you rebalanced after each 'winning' year, from 2003 onward, you would still have gotten smashed in 2008.

*But — and this is important! — you would have pocketed some of the 125%, 42%, 57% and 75% profits beforehand.*

In addition to that, your total position in 2008 would have been reduced and, therefore, you would have 'lost' less. We've developed a strategy that would have ensured you were not investing in Turkey in 2007 anyway, thus avoiding 2008, but that's not the point we're making here. Indeed, being the astute investor by understanding mean reversion — and making sure you buy low and sell high — you could have placed more in Turkey at the bottom of 2008 and start of 2009.

And that nearly doubles your money again on the rebound. Rebalancing forces you to buy low and to sell high and means that you can become very wealthy over time by avoiding significant losses.

**FIGURE 14.1 – EMERGING MARKETS RETURNS**

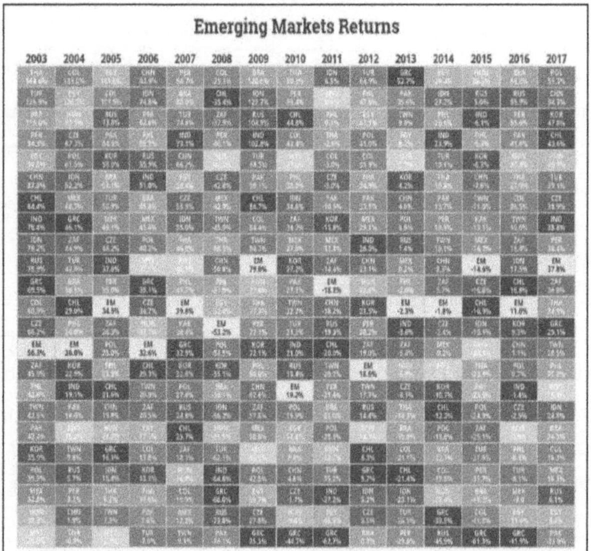

Source: Novel Investor

This example is not just cherry-picking to prove a point. We're simply pointing out that because of the interplay between momentum and mean reversion, you must take profits at the highs and put them back in at the lows. It also shows that even markets that have performed very badly, on average, over a long period of time, can still have periods where they perform outstandingly well!

Remember a static/passive buy-and-hold approach sees you receive the long-term average — which we know is not a recipe for investment success — and we're actually misled by thinking the average compounds at 7% or 8% per year. And markets such as Greece or Turkey have delivered terrible annual returns over the past 15 years.

Only in approximately 10 years has the ASX returned the average 8–10%.

*In all other years, the returns are either higher or lower than the average.*

And that variability can greatly affect your investment returns. Here are some other points to consider, and to show why rebalancing is critical. The first is the effect on a portfolio of negative numbers and compound returns. For example, if you make 20%, then lose 20%, the average return appears to be zero ... but you lose 4% because of the way investing works.

Try the numbers for yourself.

Buy at $100 and make 20%, then you have $120.

Now lose 20% from there, and you go back to $96.

You do not go back to the original $100, even though the 'average' return appears to be zero.

*So when you make a handsome profit, take it.*

This dynamic works in reverse too. For a 20% loss, the required gain to get you back to break even is 25%. It's the same problem whether the positive or the negative return occurs first.

A 25% gain is wiped out by 20% loss. Now another trouble-some factor is known as the *range of returns*. As the range of returns becomes more dispersed from the average, the compounded return declines. For example, three consecutive periods of 5% returns is greater than any other sequence that averages 5%.

5% +5% + 5% equals 15, with an average of 5%.

But if you vary that ever so slightly, say with 6% + 5% + 4% = 5% average, notice how the compounding annual return is lower. In this case, we are just demonstrating using simple figures — but remember the range of returns can vary very considerably in the stock market.

And finally, as the variability of the returns increases (greater volatility), there is a decline in the beneficial effects of compounding returns.

9% + 5% + 1% = 5% average.

Compounded return = 4.949%.

Notice that the greater the differences year to year, the less money you end up receiving.

Because of the sequence of returns, you must rebalance.

## Rebalancing in practice

Let us show you how rebalancing can add considerable value to your portfolio performance. Whether you decide to do it weekly, monthly, quarterly or annually, the important point is to reassess your portfolio and do as Mandelbrot says — take profits! It might provide some comfort to realise that the finance industry and fund managers rebalance quite regularly, and they use rebalancing as part of managing your superannuation portfolio.

That is why they have target weights for each asset class. So when the asset class — say equities — expands above the allocation, they rebalance to bring the allocation back within their mandated limits. There are a few ways you can think about rebalancing.

You can rebalance on a percentage basis or a time basis.

*We generally prefer to rebalance on a calendar or time basis because it's emotionally harder to do it when you have bragging rights attached to a winner.*

Being up 50% on an investment, it can be so tempting to hold on and reach 60% ... and then because things keep going well, you become tempted to hold again. Recency bias kicks in and you decide to hold the winner for a longer period of time or hesitate to commit more funds to a 'loser'. The systematic approach is invaluable here.

As we show below, the ideal investments are those that are uncorrelated — meaning they have no relationship and a movement in one (e.g. stocks), does not affect the other (e.g. cash). In what seems rather paradoxical, rebalancing between stocks and cash can significantly outperform a buy-and-hold strategy. At this point I see many faces turning ugly.

Cash!

*'Gee, it's getting like 2% or something.'*

This may be true (at the moment), but don't be afraid to hold cash.

Or, if you have a mortgage, an offset account can work just as well.

Because the stock market ebbs and flows, you will periodically have opportunities to put that capital to work and compound your wealth at a greater rate.

Charlie Munger, Buffett's sidekick, relates a great story, as frustrating as it can be:

*'You have $10,000 and a choice: invest today and earn 7% for 10 years.*

*Or leave your money in cash earning 4% for four years, and then invest in a stock and earn 10% for the next six years.*

*After 10 years, you would have 16% more money — more than $1,000 — if you simply sat on your cash for four years waiting for a great opportunity.*

*Waiting patiently for that 10% per annum opportunity yields dramatic results.*

*But you must have the cash in the first place to be able to capitalise on the great opportunities.'*

Hopefully, we know what you're thinking:

### 'OK, I get it, but how much do I take out or put in?'

Here's one simple method (though it's not the only method).

If you do this with mean-reverting indexes — such as the ASX in Australia or other country indexes — you will succeed in generating greater returns than buy-and-hold over the longer term.

Start with a simple stylised example portfolio, with $5,000 in stocks and $5,000 in cash.

You decide that you will commit to a 50/50 rebalance, and so your very simplified portfolio looks like this.

You make a terrible mistake, and your initial $5,000 in stocks have halved, and so your total portfolio is now $7,500, with $2,500 in stocks and $5,000 in cash.

Now let's rebalance (at your chosen interval) to 50/50 with $3,750 in both stocks and cash.

So you need to use $1,250 of your cash to buy more stocks.

Now you are back to 50/50 again.

The next time to rebalance comes, and the value of your stocks have doubled, so now you have a portfolio value of $11,250, with $7,500 in stocks and $3,750 in cash.

Now here's the nice part.

After the stock market has lost 50% and then gone up 100%, the stock market index is the same as the starting point.

Yet you have made $1,250 profit over the two trades while the buy-and-hold investor has made nothing, before accounting for dividends and inflation.

Of course, the balance doesn't always have to be 50/50.

If stock markets become cheap, then you might go to 70/30 or even 80/20.

Take some time to think carefully about this.

Run through some scenarios, for both bull markets and bear markets.

When applied systematically, rebalancing is a very powerful tool and concept.

Not only can it help you to reduce risk by forcing you to buy low and take profits, it can also improve your returns over time.

Remember the market goes up roughly 70% of the time, so taking profits in the good times means more to invest in the down times.

Simply rebalance between the value of stocks and cash. This is the magic of rebalancing, which essentially forces you to buy low and sell high. Of course, this is a simple and stylised example. But the concept is critically important to investing safely and successfully through the cycles. The idea is to maintain a specific balance (which you're comfortable with) between two asset classes.

In this case, let's say it's between cash and stocks. As the example above shows, 50/50 is a very simple place to start, as it leaves you plenty to inject if the market falls. This may seem to be a lot of cash, but if you want to, you can adjust to your personal preference of 60% stocks, 40% cash.

Or when stocks are cheap, you could hold a 70/30% portfolio, meaning $1,400 in stocks and $600 in cash.

In accordance with our other principles, we often let the market valuation and market cycles tell us what the starting balance should be.

> *In a low market when prices are cheap,*
> *you may wish to start with say 70% in stocks*
> *and 30% in cash.*

Again, simply rebalance to those percentage weightings and ... hey, presto! A simple yet effective way to build wealth safely and consistently through rebalancing. Don't be afraid to take profits. We have shown you how simple rebalancing is and the value it can add to your portfolio.

Remember the old Bernard Baruch saying:

*'I made my money by selling too soon.'*

# CHAPTER 15

# BRINGING IT ALL TOGETHER

## Review thoughts

OK, so you've made it this far, and you think you may now be ready. Hopefully, you will have grasped the importance of having an overall investment philosophy from the sections where we have discussed risk, personality, and stock market patterns. The 8 Timeless Principles are there to assist you in developing a systematic approach.

It's important to review both the thought and action principles to see if your portfolio is holding up.

> *No investment strategy will always outperform everybody else.*

Though you'll inevitably experience both better times and periods when you underperform, having a solid investment philosophy with principles will stand you in good stead throughout your investing journey. Developing a checklist can seem like a chore. But a checklist and a system are necessary to help jog your memory to see if you have forgotten anything.

Atul Gawande in his book *The Checklist Manifesto* showed how doctors reduced the number of people dying from surgery via simple procedures such as checking that hands had been washed[1]. The problem usually arises when we think we don't need a checklist because we 'have it covered'.

Often in our Next Level Wealth coaching programs, we help clients to build their own checklists. Let's give you a small *Investment Map* to get you started, which will act as a guide or checklist in your approach to investing.

## Focus first on risk

Your number one priority is to focus on risk. And by that we mean *don't lose money*. Even before you buy a stock, or a property, think about risk. Focus on how the investment could lose money.

*Are you adopting a systematic approach?*
*Are you buying at the right time in the market cycle?*
*Are you buying low?*
*Are you allocating a specified amount of your capital?*
*Are you holding some cash against it?*

Often investors make the mistake of simply deciding to buy a stock and ignoring any potential warning signs (like a company that has a very high debt level and a shrinking cash flow). Let's recap briefly on the 8 timeless principles, and how you can apply them to building your wealth safely.

## Principle #1: Systematic investing

Remember much success in investing is about the application of a formula. Your aim should be to develop a systematic approach. The seven remaining principles should form part of your investment thoughts and processes. When you see yourself drifting away from your system, as invariably you will, ask yourself *why* you are stepping away from your system.

If your system makes you a successful investor, then why would you choose another approach? If an investment appears to have a lot going for it, then it should fit the criteria of your system.

If not, then let it pass. Remember you're not compelled to do anything, and there will be plenty of investment opportunities over your lifetime.

## Principle #2: Personality/decision-making

You may be surprised to know how many people make investment decisions without adequate research and allow their emotions to dictate their decision-making. It's important to understand your own personality and motivations as this is probably the number one cause of bad decisions. Try to avoid buying what's popular or in the daily headlines — because once it's there, then it's no longer cheap.

Always aim to ask yourself, am I using what Kahneman calls 'System 2 thinking': calm, considered and rational?

*Am I making this decision in a cool and calm environment?*

Don't rush. Take your time, as the stock or investment property will still be there tomorrow.

## Principle #3: Market cycles/mean reversion

Remember mean reversion is a dominant feature of stocks, property and other asset classes. They all cycle, and so you should start by focussing on looking for the depressed stocks or the ones that most folks don't want to know about.

This is where you can make outsized returns. Ask yourself where are we in the market cycle?

*Is the CAPE ratio high or low?*

*Is it trending down or looking to go higher?*

Let the numbers rather than the stories or media narratives guide you. Numbers have a much higher degree of success in predicting the future than narratives.

## Principle #4: The risk hierarchy

Remember to focus on high probability investments that reduce your chances of a loss. We believe you can achieve excellent returns by using ETFs rather than trying to focus on picking individual companies.

If you must pick companies, stick to the larger end of the market and choose those that provide a dividend and have done so for years.

Remember the tortoise beats the hare over the long term. Slow and steady wins the race.

## Principle #5: Asset allocation

Don't be greedy! If a stock is low, it can go lower (and unpopular stocks often do). So plan accordingly. Asset allocation is an important principle that helps you avoid losing … having a conservative allocation is fine.

Building wealth is more about small and consistent wins than big wins and big losses. Start with a 50/50 allocation between stocks and cash and work from there. This will give you some comfort if the stock falls after your initial purchase.

## Principle #6: Buy low, sell high!

When you look to buy a stock or other investment, check to see if the price is low based on the average earnings over time.

Stocks or property can look cheap, but the cheapness comes from appearing to see a rosy future predicated on nothing going wrong and ignoring mean reversion.

How, then, do we buy low, sell high?

1. Look for markets/sectors/styles that are out of favour. You can buy the whole country, a sector, or style via ETFs (or individual companies if that's your bent). A cheap market usually implies that individual companies within the asset class are cheap. Now, that does not mean you can buy any old company, but usually large systemic companies with modest debt levels is a good place to start.

2. Remember there are two parts to this equation — buying and selling — so start a rebalancing process after 12 months when the tax implications are positive and then repeat the 'buy low' process again. Remember profits are not realised until you sell.

3. Mean reversion and market cycles (via the CAPE ratio) should be at the forefront of your mind, so don't get psyched out if the

stock falls further. If you have a solid asset allocation plan, then this should not be an issue.

Remember most stock returns revert towards the long-term average — and many companies don't make money over the long term — so take profits and avoid a cardinal sin of many investors — getting greedy.

## Principle #7: Diversification

Make sure you are not too exposed to one investment or asset class. Yes, stocks may be cheap at certain times, but that doesn't mean you can throw away the book and go crazy. Make sure you take a global approach and invest in several markets, and across several sectors. You can always adjust your asset allocation from 50/50 to 70/30 to accommodate an opportunity that appears to provide a high expected return.

Aim to invest in:

1. **Developed markets** — look for the laggards, not the winners. They revert;
2. **Emerging markets** — as for developed markets, look for the recent underperformers. The big returns come when the whole emerging markets' countries have been out of favour;
3. **Sectors** — look at the sectors that everyone presently hates. And use ETFs to buy them as they will come back into favour. All sectors fluctuate through the broad market cycle, and within their own business cycle; and
4. **Styles** — for example buying value ETFs or growth ETFs when they are low.

## Principle #8: Rebalancing

Rebalancing is a critical component of your investment success, so don't ignore it. When to rebalance should be approached systematically, and you can decide that by considering how much time and effort you want to put into managing your investments. As you become more experienced you may adjust it but be mindful of market cycles. You will need to rebalance more in a secular bear market where the volatility will eat away at your gains.

### Take profits!

At the start, try to rebalance to a 50/50 proportion. But your approach should be to let the market indicators such as the CAPE ratio dictate your positions. So with a low CAPE ratio of say five, you may decide not to rebalance until it hits 10, rather than rebalance earlier. This can be a valid approach, especially for those investments that are extremely cheap to start with. This should see you steadily take profits or adding to your position if it falls.

Remember the sequence of returns. It's critically important to acknowledge the role of the sequence of returns. It should help you realise to take profits when they are there.

## Some final additional points

Remember no one is perfect, including us!

You cannot make every investment a success, simply because there are other people and luck involved.

1. You will never get to master the art of perfect timing. You'll probably buy too early or sell too early. So be it — it's just an accepted part of investing;
2. Think about the long term — this doesn't mean simply buy and hold but accept that the effects of randomness will apply often. You won't always get the benefit or costs of currency fluctuations etc. They will usually wash out over time; and
3. Think like a contrarian — while we understand it can 'feel' difficult, the most successful investors are the ones who swim against the tide.

The wealthy buy low and sell high, they stick to their system, and they make the big decisions when others hesitate.

That is how they built their wealth.

It did not come from being like everyone else.

# CHAPTER 16

# WHAT NEXT?

## Building your 3 Wealth Wells

Steve:

*When I retired, I was forced to consider more carefully how I should manage my money. There were a few things that surprised me.*

*The first was that, obviously, you don't receive a cheque or payday every week or month with the same amount! This tended to confuse me a little as some weeks I would make my "wage" in the stock market only to 'lose it' the very next week.*

*The stock market fluctuates, and so in order to avoid any concerns about whether I was making a wage or not, I decided to use a technique called broad framing.*

The concept of broad framing is quite simple. In those weeks that the stock market declined, I would check my portfolio and be consoled by reminding myself that the stock market fluctuates, and so it would probably bounce back.

Secondly, it was extremely unlikely that I was going to run out of money given that I generally don't get too carried away on the spending side. I lead a pretty modest lifestyle, and so that allayed any fears of running out of money.

Thirdly, broad framing my wealth meant looking at my total wealth and telling myself that the stock market decline means I 'lost' 0.01% of my total wealth.

*This showed me how silly it was to worry about losses, and in most cases, the losses were temporary rather than permanent.*

So here is what we call 'The Three Wealth Wells'.

It's exactly how we manage our money. While we all live in the here and now, at the same time we need to consider our future and its requirements.

At Next Level Wealth, we think about money in the following way.

We all need liquid money for the here and now, including daily or weekly living expenses such as utility bills, groceries, eating out, etc. Next, you need some funds for the intermediate period — for the two- to five-year horizon. This wealth well will cover expenses like your holidays, school fees, car upgrades and so on.

These funds also need to be reasonably liquid — such as in stocks or cash — and can be actively managed to maximise returns safely. And lastly, you need to consider your longer-term financial needs such as retirement spending and handing on a legacy for your loved ones. For many people, this might include their superannuation, and potentially a range of other long-term investments, such as property, or large systemic companies that pay a long track record of paying healthy dividends.

As you can see, we think the different timeframes require different strategies.

The key is to actively manage your money to make sure that across each of these three timeframes you have enough money.

## Well 1: living costs (0 to 12 months)

**Well 1** needs to comprise liquid assets, cash flow, and easy access combined with low transactional costs. The Next Level Wealth trading strategy based on our unique investment philosophy in combination with the 8 Timeless Principles, is designed specifically for this purpose.

This strategy aims to deliver cash flow like a weekly or fortnightly wage, taking an active daily approach to stock market investing with a minimum of effort.

## Well 2: liquid investments (two to five years)

**Well 2** can focus on the medium term: school fees, more kids, car upgrades, and holidays.

This well of capital should ideally be a mixture of stocks and cash.

As we have shown through this book, our Next Level Wealth ETF strategy involves using our investment philosophy and the 8 Timeless Principles for selecting and managing a portfolio of ETFs that meet the strategy's criteria.

Normal holding periods can be anywhere from 12 months to five years, with annual systematic rebalancing.

## Well 3: legacy and longer term (lifetime)

For **Well 3**, the longer timeframe is focused on building wealth and your capital via compound growth.

This can be done via a mix of the major asset classes. The stock market focus here tends to be on larger companies that have an established track record of paying dividends.

These stocks are bought when the opportunity arises for higher than average future returns.

*We always look to hold a portion of cash to allow us to take advantage when great investment opportunities arise.*

If you like property, then Well 3 can also comprise some long-term property investments in great locations that you never plan to sell. These longer-term investments can ideally go on compounding for as long as you live and can form part of your legacy.

*Note: Self-managed superannuation funds (SMSFs) tend to be a tax-effective vehicle for many people planning to invest in the stock market for the long term.*

*Speak to your financial advisor and/or accountant to understand SMSF rules.*

## Stocks versus property (or other asset classes)

There's no greater debate among investors as to whether stocks or property is the better investment. For some reason, many people seem to take sides and never the twain shall meet. Some see stocks as a casino and considerably riskier than property.

Others hold a different view. When you look at investments with a dispassionate eye and you understand the 8 Timeless Principles, you see that it is not an either/or question.

> *Astute investors realise that you can make money*
> *and build wealth in both stocks and property.*
> *It depends on what you invest in and when.*

Remember, the 8 Timeless Principles are applicable to property as much as they are to stocks.

If we understand market cycles, then there will be times throughout your investing life that stocks will be superior, and at other times property will outperform. Given the benefits of diversification, we see that holding both stocks and property can be a sensible approach for many people.

Using our 8 Timeless Principles means you should assess any investment — be it property or stocks — on what the expected return is and where you are in the market cycle. Generally, people are more emotional about property because it is our home, and everyone must live somewhere.

There are some beautiful looking properties, and if you see a grand property in an equally attractive location, then that can be a lot more emotive than an electronic entry showing that you own 100 shares of Commonwealth Bank, for example. We've both held a long-term interest and passion for all things economics.

After 20 years as an investor, Steve prefers stocks.

Steve has had property investments over the years, but he says he is 'a stocks guy' at heart.

Pete likes both asset classes but has ended up 'top heavy' in property because of the extra leverage that can be deployed in that asset class. We believe that stocks can help to offer you a faster path to true financial independence. That does not mean that property can't build your wealth.

We believe that an initial property purchase can get you on the bottom rung of the wealth ladder. Indeed, most people have a high proportion of their wealth tied up in property.

What follows are some of the reasons to consider stocks as investments. Homes are not really an investment in the same way that stocks are.

You must live somewhere, and so property is not really an investment in the sense that you can't 'cash in' to take the profit. Of course you can downsize, but this may require making some sacrifices like a smaller property or a different location. Or you could redraw some equity if the bank allows you to. There are other reasons why holding some stocks can be preferable.

■ You can't sell a bedroom to capture some of the accumulated profit as you can with stocks.

■ Any property usually requires a large initial outlay of capital and a sizable loan.

Although some people won't see it this way, you are essentially leveraging up, which increases your risk of losing. Just saying that it's for the long term doesn't necessarily wash.

If you manage to pay $100,000 less for a property, then over 25 years that saving would be extremely large because you only borrow, say, $400K not $500K. Paying less interest on $100,000 over 25 years is a considerable saving. You don't have to leverage to start building wealth via stocks.

■ As Steve is prone to saying, BHP never calls to tell me the taps are leaking, or the dishwasher is broken.

Property maintenance can eat away at the net returns.

- Compounding returns is harder because you have a generally high-cost asset that has high transaction costs before purchasing another property (you can borrow against an existing property but again that is increasing your risk).
- The liquidity of stocks is superior to that of property.

Stocks can be sold at the click of a button and at relatively low cost.

If the stock market offers future low returns, then you can quickly change investments, and as we encourage you, to look to other global markets for cheap stocks. Holding investment properties overseas in another country can be quite difficult in understanding local rules and regulations.

- Large transaction costs — as any property investor will tell you, the transaction costs of buying and selling a property are very significant.

In our Next Level Wealth program, we have many clients who have done well from property but get to the point of changing their lifestyle thanks to their investments.

They discover that they either need to wait a long time to realise the capital gains (pay off the loan before you get to keep the full rent returns), or they need to continue to leverage up and buy more investment properties in order to build wealth.

*That is why we believe property can get you on the wealth ladder, but a transition to holding some stocks makes sense for people wanting to experience true financial independence.*

## It's not that hard, honestly ...

Pete and Steve hold qualifications in finance, accounting, financial planning, real estate and more. But we both understood that universities and diplomas often teach you how to be a financial advisor. But what the qualifications teach is not always in the client's best interest. You are sometimes taught how to manage and develop client portfolios in order to generate fees or your wage.

> *Most of our clients who undertake our mentoring programs find that it is not that hard to understand markets and to manage a reasonably sizable portfolio.*

They are surprised once we discuss the philosophy and principles at just how easy it is. The finance industry makes it appear difficult because that is how they generate their salaries. Remember what we outlined in the section on why you should manage your own money — you will save a lot of fees over your investing lifetime!

## Your ideal day

We often get the question from clients: how come you have enough money to retire but you are still mentoring people in stocks and property? One answer is that you must do something!

One of the surprising elements to retirement is that the days can be long, and there are many hobbies that you can do for an hour or so ... but not for 16 hours a day, every day.

Our days tend to be quite varied.

Steve:

*I usually do a range of activities each day.*

*I look after my young children.*

*I love reading, so I try to read for at least 1–2 hours a day, and usually at the local coffee shop.*

*This is then followed by doing some exercise, which means either weight training or walking in the nearby park.*

*Then it's playing guitar or playing golf.*

*Of course, there are clients to mentor too.*

*But most days I simply look at stock markets, I search the web for articles, and read many daily papers about politics, economics and social issues.*

*You'd be amazed at how often many investors fail to incorporate politics into their assessment of risk when investing. But if someone asked what the major benefit is, there are two that come immediately to mind.*

*Firstly, I enjoy the freedom of being my own boss.*

*And, secondly, there is the psychic income obtained from teaching and seeing people get great results.*

*We simply enjoy teaching people how to invest and not lose money.*

Modern life with small children is hectic for most parents. A major benefit of financial independence is being able to relax and take care of children minus the stress of trying to manage this as well as a job. We can attend all school sports days, swimming carnivals, and even contribute to helping at the school tuck shop if we feel like it.

## Let us be your millionaire mentors

Between us, we have nearly 50 years of investing experience. We cover the two major asset classes that most people invest in — stocks and property.

We both have university qualifications (among a range of other qualifications, Pete is a Fellow of the Institute of Chartered Accountants, and Steve has a Bachelor of Science and a Masters of Applied Finance).

We have spent thousands of hours studying for university and other finance qualifications, and thousands of dollars on reading books regarding economics, investing, finance and accounting.

Between us, we spend perhaps 60 to 80 hours each week reading books, reading articles, and researching to get answers to our questions. And we're constantly thinking about how to become better investors, and how to improve our courses to make it easier for people to manage their own money and build their own wealth.

## What next?

Thank you for reading our book.

Now it's down to you.

> *Successful and safe investing is not that hard … honestly.*

As you have seen in this book, the principles of smart investing can be surprisingly simple.

Buy stocks when they are cheap and sell them for a profit.

Diversify and rebalance your portfolio to manage risk.

And reduce the risk of permanent losses by using ETFs.

If you're interested in learning more, or if you have any questions, please get in touch with us at the following email addresses:

pete@gonextlevelwealth.com.au

steve@gonextlevelwealth.com.au

# REFERENCES

**Chapter 2 — Hey, where's my yacht?**

1. *The Little Book of Common-Sense Investing: The Only Way to Guarantee Your Fair Share of Market Returns*, John C. Bogle (Wiley & Sons, 2007)
2. *ibid.*
3. credit to Alan Kohler of *InvestSMART* for having regularly highlighted this point in his analysis
4. Alan Kohler, The Conversation, *Superannuation is too costly, so bill me*
https://theconversation.com/
superannuation-is-too-costly-so-bill-me-25199

**Chapter 3 — Why you should manage your own money**

1. www.novelinvestor.com

**Chapter 4 — The solution: an investment philosophy**

1. *Irrational Exuberance*, Robert J. Shiller (Princeton University Press, 2000)
2. *ibid.*
3. *ibid.*

**Chapter 5 — Market cycles**

1. *Mastering the Market Cycle: Getting the Odds on Your Side*, Howard Marks (HMH Books, 2018)

**Chapter 8 — Principle #2: Personality/decision-making**

1. Enneagram Institute, www.enneagraminstitute.com

## Chapter 9 — Principle #3: Mean reversion (& macro valuations)

1. *Irrational Exuberance*, Robert J. Shiller (Princeton University Press, 2000)
2. *Thinking Fast and Slow*, Daniel Kahneman (Farrar, Strauss, and Giroux, 2011)
3. See Michael Mauboussin's research on Return on Invested Capital (ROIC)
4. Greenwald et al. pages 19—25
5. ibid.
6. *Contrarian Investment Strategies: The Next Generation*, David Drehman
7. *Security Analysis*, Ben Graham

## Chapter 10 — Principle #4: The risk hierarchy

1. *The Black Swan: The Impact of the Highly Improbable*, Nassim Nicholas Taleb (Random House, 2007)

## Chapter 12 — Principle #6: Buy low, sell high!

1. *The Intelligent Investor*, Benjamin Graham (Harper & Bros, 1949).
2. *Value Investing: Tools and Techniques for Intelligent Investment*, James Montier (Wiley, 2012)

## Chapter 15 — Bringing it all together

1. *The Checklist Manifesto: How to Get Things Right*, Atul Gawande (Henry Holt, 2009)

# APPENDIX

# ENNEAGRAM ASSESSMENT AND INVESTMENT MAPS

## ENNEAGRAM TYPE ASSESSMENT

While we might not fit snugly into one personality type, each of us will have dominant personality type (sometimes with a second personality type 'wing').

When running our Next Level Wealth coaching programs, we have found that the most common applicants are types 3, 5 and 7.

That's because these are the personality types that place some level of importance on money.

Choose the one type that is most applicable to you from the nine Types below:

## Type 1 (reformer)

I believe money is important, and I can be quite serious about money.

I hold strong views about money, what is right and wrong, what is acceptable and what is not.

I usually put a limited amount of effort into money matters.

I try to live within my means and not be too greedy or excessive.

I generally don't like debt, but I am comfortable borrowing for a home or a car.

I enjoy spending on nice/expensive goods because they are worth it.

I do tend to compare myself with others in seeing what material things they have.

## Type 2 (helper)

Money does not interest me very much, and I like to spend it to help other people before spending it on myself.

Spending on myself seems a bit selfish, and I don't like asking any other people for money.

I am generally optimistic and believe things will probably work out in the end.

Money is not a great motivator for me, so I spend a limited amount of time and effort thinking about it.

## Type 3 (achiever) — money brings significance

I enjoy achieving my goals, and money is one of the ways that validates my approach to life.

Being money conscious, I work hard to develop my skills, and I am not afraid to work hard to achieve my monetary goals.

I can budget reasonably easily.

I am happy to borrow and paying off any debt is usually not a problem.

I am happy to study money.

## Type 4 (individualist)

Money is not a motivating force for me, and so I don't think it can deliver a meaningful life.

I can be creative about earning, spending and investing money, but things I spend money on have to have some personal meaning to me.

Although I'm not that interested in money, I do tend to have expensive taste and overspend.

Money is not something that is exciting to me, so I don't really make any effort in managing money.

## Type 5 (thinker, analyser, investigator) — money means security

I am generally self-sufficient, and so I generally minimise the need for money.

I don't really need that much money to survive, so I don't place a great deal of effort in earning a lot of money.

I do think money is useful for allowing me to be more self-sufficient.

I don't really worry at all about what others have or 'keeping up with the Joneses'.

I don't think too much about money.

## Type 6 (loyalist)

I generally believe money helps in gaining security, and while I can occasionally splurge, most of the time I am reasonably frugal and try not to spend too much.

Even though I may have some debt, it makes me a bit nervous.

I like 'bargains' and think getting value for money is more important than buying expensive products.

I put in a certain amount of effort regarding money but probably not as much as some other people.

## Type 7 (adventurer) — money allows freedom

Money is important to me because it presents opportunities and can fulfil my needs.

I think money is a way to increase my options and freedom.

I generally don't limit my spending or devote too much time to thinking about a budget, and when I buy something I can have a budget in mind, but I am happy to spend more if I like a product.

Having some savings is good as it can provide me with more options. If I really think about it, I am happy to study how to increase my wealth.

## Type 8 (challenger)

I want what I want and think that if you work hard, you should be able to get it.

I like to be the master of my own destiny and control my money.

I prefer to focus on making more money rather than reducing my spending.

I think budgets are restrictive, and if I make a lot of money I should be able to spend a lot of it too.

I am happy to put in effort for the sake of money.

## Type 9 (peacemaker)

Money provides me with comfort and peace of mind.

I'm self-reliant and financially responsible, and I don't spend too much on myself.

Money is not overly interesting to me, and so I don't work too hard or study investing too much.

It's not really a motivating force for me, and so I don't really spend a great deal of time and effort on money.

I have a relaxed attitude towards money, and I don't think about improving my finances.

I am happy to let my partner or a professional manage the finances.

### Your free investment roadmap

Hopefully, you will have identified one personality type that describes you best.

You can now email us for you free investment roadmap:

pete@gonextlevelwealth.com.au

steve@gonextlevelwealth.com.au

This helps your development as an investor because you will immediately be able to recognise your strengths and weaknesses, and some of your potential foibles and pitfalls.

We all have our own biases, and an Investment Map can help you to recognise and avoid them.

# FURTHER RESOURCES AND RECOMMENDED READING

## Systematic investing
*How to Make $1,000,000 in the Stock Market*, Robert Lichello
*The 52-Week Low Formula*, Luke L. Wiley
*Beating the Dow*, Michael O'Higgins
*Value Averaging*, Michael E Edleson
*Buffettology*, Mary Buffett and David Clark

## Mean reversion and market cycles
*Mastering the Market Cycle*, Howard Marks
*The Most Important Thing*, Howard Marks
*Deep Value*, Tobias Carlisle
*The Success Equation*, Michael Mauboussin
*Unexpected Returns*, Ed Easterling
*Probable Outcomes*, Ed Easterling
*Anatomy of the Bear*, Russell Napier
*The Little Book of Stock Market Cycles*, Jeff Hirsch
*Bull*, Maggie Mahar
*Wisdom on Value Investing*, Gabriel Wisdom

## Risk hierarchy
*Fooled by Randomness*, Nassim Nicholas Taleb
*The Black Swan*, Nassim Nicholas Taleb
*Antifragile*, Nassim Nicholas Taleb
*The (Mis)Behavior of Markets*, Benoit Mandelbrot and
    Richard Hudson
*Against the Gods*, Peter Bernstein
*Deep Risk*, William J. Bernstein

*Red-Blooded Risk*, Aaron Brown
*Expected Returns*, Antti Ilmanen
*Risk and the Smart Investor*, David Martin

## Rebalancing
*Stock Trading Riches*, Praveen Puri
*How to Make $1,000,000 in The Stock Market*, Robert Lichello

## Buy low, sell high
*The 52-Week-Low Formula*, Luke L. Wiley
*Yes, You Can Time the Market*, Stein & DeMuth
*Here Are the Customers' Yachts*, Jeffery Weber
*It's When You Sell That Counts*, Donald Cassidy
*The Little Book That Beats the Market*, Joel Greenblatt
*Contrarian Investment Strategies*, David Dreman
*John Neff on Investing*, John Neff

## Asset allocation
*The ETF Book*, Richard A. Ferri
*Templeton's Way with Money*, Alasdair Nairn and Jonathan Davis
*The Power of Passive Investing*, Richard A. Ferri
*Global Value*, Meb Faber
*The Best Investment Writing*, Meb Faber
*Dual Momentum Investing*, Gary Antonacci
*Millennial Money*, Patrick O'Shaughnessy
*Global Asset Allocation*, Meb Faber
*The Intelligent Asset Allocator*, Willian Bernstein

## Psychology
*Personality Types (Enneagram)*, Riso & Hudson
*The Complete Enneagram*, Beatrice Chestnutt
*The Behavioural Investor*, Daniel Crosby
*Thinking Fast and Slow*, Daniel Kahneman
*Seeking Wisdom*, Peter Bevelin

*Irrational Exuberance*, Robert Shiller
*The Art of Contrary Thinking*, Humphrey Neil
*Why You Win or Lose*, Fred. C. Kelly
*Social Physics*, Mark Buchanan
*The Successful Self*, Dorothy Rowe
*What Investors Really Want*, Meir Statman
*How Emotions Are Made*, Lisa Feldman Barrett

## General reading
*The Only Three Questions That Count*, Ken Fisher
*Stocks for the Long Run*, Jeremy Siegel
*Bulls, Bears and a Croupier*, Matthew Kidman
*Forecast*, Mark Buchanan
*Critical Mass*, Phillip Ball
*Scale*, Geoffrey West
*What Works on Wall Street*, James O'Shaughnessy
*Ubiquity*, Mark Buchanan
*Beat the Crowd*, Ken Fisher
*Markets Never Forget*, Ken Fisher
*The Intelligent Investor*, Ben Graham
*The Snowball*, Alice Schroeder
*The Rediscovered Ben Graham*, Janet Lowe
*Excess Returns*, Fredrick Vanhaverbeke
*Warren Buffett and The Interpretation of Financial Statements*,
    Mary Buffett and David Clark
*Value Investing*, Bruce. C. Greenwald
*Competition Demystified*, Bruce C. Greenwald

# GLOSSARY OF TERMS

**Appreciation:** the increase in value of an asset over time.

**Asset:** an item of value that could be converted into cash.

**Bull market:** a financial market where prices are either rising or are expected to rise. The opposite dynamic is known as a *bear market*, sometimes defined by prices falling by 20% or more.

**Capital growth:** like appreciation, refers to the increase in the value of an asset over time.

**Cash flow:** a snapshot of cash coming in or out of a business or your personal finances, the figure can either be positive or negative.

**Compound interest or compound growth:** a term used in business to refer to a constant rate of return. In practical terms, the 'interest on interest' makes a sum of money grow faster than you expect over time.

**Depreciation:** the decrease or fall in value of an asset over time.

**Financial advisor:** a professional qualified to give advice on money, investments, insurance, mortgages, and other financial products.

**Illiquid:** see *liquidity*.

**Income tax:** a tax imposed by the government on individuals earning income.

**Interest rate:** the amount charged, expressed as percentage of the principal, charged by a lender to a borrower. Typically expressed as an annual amount.

**Leverage:** in finance, often refers to the amount of debt used by a person or business to finance the purchase of assets or expanding a business. In a broader sense, refers to the ability to do more with less.

**Liability:** the future sacrifice of economic benefits that a person or entity is obliged to make a result of past transactions or agreements.

**Liquidity:** the degree to which an asset can be bought or sold quickly without impacting the price of the asset. An illiquid asset is not easy to sell quickly for a good price, for example.

**Passive income:** colloquially refers to income that is derived from little effort.

**Real estate:** property, generally consisting of land and buildings.

**Transaction costs:** any costs incurred in the making of a trade in a market.

**Yield:** the income returns on an investment, such as rent from real estate or dividends from stocks and shares. Typically expressed as an annual percentage rate based upon the cost of the investment.

# JOIN OUR PROGRAM

**NEXT LEVEL WEALTH**

**A unique program that explains:**
- Why you should manage your own money
- Eight key principles in investment success
- How to invest globally
- How to avoid losing money in the share market

**This program will:**
- Give you lifelong knowledge and skills which can be applied through-out your entire investing life
- Provide insights into your personality and how you can use it to your advantage when investing
- Show you how to develop a framework for applying the principles to any investment, whether it is stocks, property or bonds.
- Give you confidence to manage your own financial portfolio.
- Save you $1,000 in financial advice fees

Steve has been full time investor since 2006

Steve has a Bachelor of Science and a Masters of Applied Finance

**A simple investment program that delivers above average stock market returns**
- Show you how to understand both short and long term stock market cycles
- How to think about risk when it comes to investing and your portfolio.
- Why you don't need to pick stocks

**NEXT LEVEL WEALTH**

E: coaching@gonextlevelwealth.com.au
facebook.com/PeteWargent/
www.gonextlevelwealth.com.au

# ALSO BY PETE WARGENT

*Get a Financial Grip: A Simple Plan for Financial Freedom* (Big Sky, Sydney, 2012). Rated in the Top 10 Finance books of 2012 by *Money Magazine* and Dymocks.

*'Pete Wargent gives you a simple plan for achieving financial freedom at any age.'*

CHRIS GRAY, AUTHOR AND TV PRESENTER OF *YOUR MONEY YOUR CALL* AND CHANNEL 10'S *THE RENOVATORS*.

*Four Green Houses and a Red Hotel: New Strategies for Creating Wealth Through Property* (Big Sky, Sydney, 2013).

*'Writing a book that is new and interesting yet relevant to our changing times is a tough gig. 'But Pete Wargent, one of Australia's finest young financial commentators, achieves this in his book, sharing a wealth of information. 'I have been investing for over 40 years and read nearly every book on property ever written, yet still learned new concepts in this book.'*

MICHAEL YARDNEY, AMAZON #1 BEST-SELLING AUTHOR AND AUSTRALIA'S LEADING EXPERT IN WEALTH CREATION THROUGH PROPERTY.

*Take a Financial Leap: The 3 Golden Rules for Financial and Life Success* (Big Sky, Sydney, 2015).

*'A blueprint for escaping the rat race and achieving financial freedom … by someone who's actually managed to do it!'*

MICHAEL YARDNEY, AMAZON #1 BEST-SELLING AUTHOR AND AUSTRALIA'S LEADING EXPERT IN WEALTH CREATION THROUGH PROPERTY.

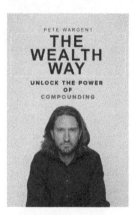

*'This a sensible, down-to-earth, well-written book about building wealth. Pete's ideas are not only easy to understand, they have the added advantage of being right: there's no doubt that the best and safest way to build wealth is to save, invest patiently, and let the power of compounding do the work. Perhaps the most surprising thing is how hard that is to do, which is why books like this are so important.'*

ALAN KOHLER, ABC NEWS AND ABC 'INSIDE BUSINESS', AND FORMER EDITOR-IN-CHIEF OF BUSINESS SPECTATOR AND EUREKA REPORT.

*'Pete is one of the very best finance writers. Do yourself a favour and get this book.'*

STEPHEN KOUKOULAS, LEADING GLOBAL ECONOMIST, MANAGING DIRECTOR OF MARKET ECONOMICS, AND FORMER SENIOR ECONOMIC ADVISOR TO PRIME MINISTER GILLARD.

# ABOUT
# THE AUTHORS

Pete Wargent is a finance and investment expert, and the co-founder of AllenWargent property buyers with offices in Sydney, Brisbane and London. He also owns an advisory business and a financial education company.

By profession, Pete trained as a Chartered Accountant in London. Having worked for top accounting institutions and listed companies, he holds a range of other top financial qualifications including being a chartered secretary and holding diplomas in Financial Planning and Applied Corporate Governance.

Pete quit his full-time job at the age of 33 having achieved financial freedom through investing in shares, index funds and investment properties. He is a keen blogger and posts his thoughts on finance, investment, the markets and much more besides daily on his free blog at petewargent.blogspot.com.

Pete is the author of the 2012 investment book *Get a Financial Grip: A Simple Plan for Financial Freedom,* which was rated as one of the top 10 finance books of 2012 by Dymocks and *Money Magazine.*

Pete is also the author of 2013 property investment book *Four Green Houses and a Red Hotel: New Strategies for Creating Wealth Through Property.*

In 2014, Pete's third book was released, *Take a Financial Leap: The Three Golden Rules for Financial and Life Success.*

Pete's fourth book, *The Wealth Way: Unlock the Power of Compounding* was published internationally in 2017.

Stephen Moriarty has a Masters of Applied Finance.

Steve is not just a theorist, however, and he has been a full-time investor in the markets for more than 15 years.

A widely read investor, Steve developed his unique 8 timeless principles investment approach over more than a decade and a half in the markets.

Steve lives in Brisbane, Australia.